Search for the Soul

Search for the Soul

By the Editors of Time-Life Books

TIME-LIFE BOOKS, ALEXANDRIA, VIRGINIA

Photographed before his face was weathered by thirty years of prospecting in Arizona's desert, James Kidd looks fresh and dapper. The eccentric loner touched off a lengthy courtroom search for the human soul. Before disappearing in 1949, Kidd wrote a rough, homemade will (right), requesting that his sizable estate be used to scientifically prove the existence of the soul.

Phoenix arizona

this is my first and only will and is dated the second day in January 1946. I have no, heirs have not been married in my life, too after all my funeral expenses have been paid and to one hundred dollars to some preacher of the gospital to say fare well at my grave sell all my property which is all in cash and stocks with E. F. Hutton Co Phoenix some in safety box, and have this balance money to go in a reserach or some scientific proof of a soul of the human body which leaves at death I think in time their can be a Photograph of soul leaving the human at death

James Kidd

(dated 2nd January 1946)

Symbols of the Soul

Swirling down only to reverse and uncoil, the spiral with its endless cycle has intrigued humanity from primitive times until the present. Spirals have been used as symbols in numerous cultures throughout the world, from ancient Egypt and Europe to South America to islands of the South Pacific. They have appeared on pottery, coins, and seals, and in cathedrals, mosaics, rock carvings, earth drawings, and even tattoos. Spirals in slightly altered form, as mazes and labyrinths, have been almost as ubiquitous.

Burial mounds in Ireland and Great Britain reveal spirals chiseled into stones and interior walls, and archaeologists have found evidence of an Egyptian royal tomb, dating from 3400 BC, that was constructed in a spiral-like labyrinthine pattern. Centuries-old turf and stone mazes have been found in England and in Scandinavia, and as far back as the fourth century AD, Christians constructed mazes on church grounds.

While the symbol's significance to early humans remains a mystery, some historians believe the unbroken windings of the helix usually had mystical significance regarding the fate of the soul. The confusing pathways of mazes, for example, may have represented the underworld, mapping a route for the soul to follow: The journey to the center of the maze represented death, and the return path symbolized rebirth. Similarly, the mazes of England and of Scandinavia apparently were once the sites of ritual dances and ceremonies exalting the earth's vernal rebirth. And in the myths of New Zealand's Maori tribe, the spiral was thought to assure the soul's passage into the afterworld.

Experts believe the early Christians may have equated the labyrinth's circuitous route with the arduous road to salvation, an idea not unlike one that existed in ancient Greece. Some scholars interpret the Greek myth in which the Minotaur, a bull-headed monster confined within a labyrinth, is slain by the hero Theseus as a metaphor for triumph over death.

On the Mediterranean island of Malta, spirals decorate the prehistoric temple of Hal Tarxien, a place once dedicated to the worship of an ancient fertility goddess.

CHAPTER 1

The Great Soul Trial

arly one chilly November morning in 1949, a seventy-year-old Arizona miner and prospector named James Kidd paused outside the door of the four-dollar-a-week shack he rented. He peered upward at the breaking dawn. A loner who lived quietly, Kidd often stood by himself this way, staring at the sky as if transported into a distant world. Sometimes, after a long shift in the copper mine where he worked, he would scramble onto the tin roof of the mine's pump house to study the stars. At those times, a half-quizzical, half-bemused expression would spread across the old man's weathered face, and his eyes would gleam beneath his battered gray fedora.

That same look must have been on Kidd's face as he put a match to his nickel cigar that November morning. Then, shifting the weight of a borrowed pickax on his shoulder, he shuffled out into the daylight. No one would ever see him again.

No one saw him that last morning, in fact, but Kidd's habits, as observed by his neighbors, tended to be as characteristic as they were spartan. His shabby dress, his frugality, his quirky way of skygazing had marked him as something of a benign eccentric. So had his reclusiveness, a trait that helped explain why, at the outset, his disappearance went almost unnoticed. As Kidd had few friends and no living relatives, it was several weeks before anyone even realized that he was missing. But in a greater scheme of things, his vanishing would not go unremarked. It would, in time, spark the oddest courtroom drama in American legal history.

A police investigation undertaken a month after the old man disappeared failed to turn up any clues or evidence of foul play, and, in time, Kidd was declared legally dead. The matter rested that way for a number of years, for it seemed there was little to distinguish Kidd's case from those of the hundreds of other people who end up missing each year. But James Kidd proved to be a man with a secret, one that was uncovered not by a police detective or a private investigator, but by a conscientious public servant named Geraldine Swift.

Several years after Kidd's disappearance, it fell to Swift, an Arizona estate-tax commissioner, to tidy up the few legal formalities connected with

CONTENTS

his apparent passing. It seemed a routine case; Swift had handled dozens of similar ones during her long career—or so she must have thought. Apparently, the old man had died intestate and without close kin. The normal procedure would be to liquidate whatever scanty assets he might have left behind and turn the money over to the state treasury as unclaimed property. But somehow the matter of the missing prospector began to hold a curious fascination for her. While leafing through the contents of a safe deposit box Kidd had kept, Swift came across a dog-eared photograph of the elderly miner, staring at the camera from beneath his wrinkled hat with an expression that seemed at once befuddled and wise. Something in that enigmatic expression intrigued her. For reasons so obscure that she herself could not articulate them, she delayed sending the case on through the usual channels. Swift decided she wanted to investigate further.

Before long, it began to appear that her instincts were well grounded. There turned up in her mail, flagged to the Kidd estate, a report from the stock brokerage firm of E. F. Hutton, outlining the liquidation of $18,000 worth of stock that had belonged to Kidd. A notation in the report said that a nearly equal amount had been deposited in a special account that represented the miner's accumulated dividends. This startling revelation was quickly followed by others.

Kidd, it seemed, had been a cautious and prudent investor and had maintained various accounts scattered among several banks and brokerage firms. During the following weeks, these institutions reported to Swift an astonishing catalog of assets. James Kidd—the tatterdemalion prospector who had dwelled in a hovel, dined in hash houses, and read borrowed newspapers—had left behind a fortune of precisely $174,065.69—quite a sizable sum by the standards of the 1960s.

At this point, several of Swift's colleagues began to share her interest in the Kidd matter. Some pressure was brought to bear on her to resolve the case. After all, there was no will. Why deprive the state of what was turning out to be a real windfall? Swift resisted, but by 1964—fifteen years after James Kidd's disappearance and more than five years after Swift first became involved with his legacy—

decisions had to be made. It was time to put paid to the old man's earthly ledger. Accompanied by her assistant and two tax auditors, Swift left her office and made her way to the underground vault of the First National Bank of Phoenix, where Kidd's files languished along with hundreds of other unclaimed accounts. At the time, the bank was undergoing extensive reconstruction, worsening working conditions in the already cramped and cluttered vault. The electricity had been shut off, so the chamber not only was thick with construction dust but also was pitch black. Threading her way by the beam of a flashlight amid the canvas bank sacks and stacked cartons, Swift took down—for the last time, she thought—the box containing Kidd's papers. Rifling through the yellowing files, she felt some sadness, as though she were saying farewell to an endearing, if nettlesome, old friend. By

the light of her flashlight she took up the ragged photograph, studying anew the ambiguous James Kidd smile that had so intrigued her for the past five years. She had grown strangely fond of the mysterious old man, and it seemed somehow unjust that the fortune he had so carefully amassed and frugally tended should simply disappear into the state treasury.

With a sigh, Swift replaced the photograph. She picked up a stack of stock receipts, which were bound with a rubber band. She was about to replace them when something fluttered free from the bundle and wafted to the floor. It was a scrap of lined notebook paper, bearing a blocky scrawl that she recognized as James Kidd's hand-

The classic design of the Troy Town turf maze on the grounds of a private home in Somerton, England, is composed of a series of seven interlocking concentric bands formed from a single, unbroken line. Believed by anthropologists to be hundreds of years old, the maze is thought to have been the scene of ritual dance processions.

A Maori tribesman of New Zealand displays spiral tattoos, thought to pay his passage to the next world. Maori legend says that when a tribesman dies, his soul meets a hag who devours the tattoos and lets him pass into the after-realm. If there are no markings, she will eat his eyes, blinding him to immortality's path.

A monkey's tail forms the shape of a spiral in this desert drawing, one of many mysterious patterns made by the Nasca people of Peru between 300 BC and AD 540. More than a hundred spirals have been discovered near Nasca, etched in the earth, chiseled into rocks, and painted on ceramics.

writing. As she scanned the contents, her eyes widened in amazement. "My first reaction," she would later recall, "was I just couldn't believe it was real; it must be a joke."

Swift called out for her coworkers, who had been examining other accounts in a different part of the vault. Training their flashlights on the bit of paper, the four read the document together. The writing was crude—the spelling spotty, and the syntax foggy—but the message was direct and clear: "Phoenix, Arizona, Jan 2nd 1946," it began, "this is my first and only will and is dated the second day in January 1946. I have no heirs have not been married in my life, after all my funeral expenses have been paid and #100. one hundred dollars to some preacher of the gospital to say fare well at my grave sell all my property which is all in cash and stocks with E F Hutton Co Phoenix some in safety box, and have this balance money to go in a research or some scientific proof of a soul of the human body which leaves at death I think in time their can be a Photograph of soul leaving the human at death." At the bottom of the page was the signature Swift knew so well from the financial documents she had so often studied over the years. "To read this in the dark room by flashlight!" she said. "I mean, everything the way it was, it was a very eerie feeling. I just sat there and thought that I just had to be dreaming. I even felt that I could have eaten it."

Swift's discovery touched off a nightmarish tangle of legalities and paperwork. Kidd did have a will after all, however informal its style or eccentric its contents. Was it valid? If not, the state might still get Kidd's money. If so, exactly what people or organizations could reasonably lay claim to the bequest? The will had been woefully imprecise on that score. As she waited several years for the legal system to begin unraveling the snarl, Swift would devote what attention she could to administering Kidd's account. Interest would accrue, and the fortune would grow.

Whatever shock and surprise Swift may have felt in that darkened bank vault, she could not possibly have foreseen the troublesome consequences of her discovery once it saw the full light of day. The controversy began immediately when the state attorney general and his staff, anticipating the will's perplexing legal implications, insisted that the rough, semiliterate, unwitnessed document could not possibly be valid. Some even suggested that it be destroyed. Better to forget the whole thing, give the money to the state, and save untold time, hassle, and paperwork. For Swift, however, the course was absolutely clear. She thought that at last she had some insight into the secretive character of the man whose quirky smile had so haunted her. In his aloneness, he had pondered deep and imponderable things and, perhaps, had come to certain conclusions that he felt a need to share. He had made his wishes known, and she would see to it that they were carried out. The will's legality, and how to honor it, were clearly matters that should be left to the courts to decide.

Legal dilemmas were trivial, in any case, compared with the larger question underlying the miner's bequest. What Kidd wanted was no more or less than confirmation of the existence of the human soul. He was challenging science to come up with concrete explanations for the greatest mystery of all, an enigma that has preoccupied humanity since the very outset of the human adventure. From the body spirits and life shadows of the primitive world to the neurological studies of modern Nobel laureates, through every great religion that has sought to wed the human essence to some greater reality, people have struggled to understand their own intangible spiritual selves.

The soul has been defined in myriad ways: as an invisible substance that animates the physical body, as an unseen essence separable from the body and surviving physical death, as consciousness, as mind, as personality. Yet the concept of soul remains somehow elusive, ineffable. Its exact nature, if in fact it does exist, may never be fully understood. Yet for many there remains no greater mission than to persist in trying to understand, since so many great ques-

Travelers to Spirit Worlds

Chief of the Norse gods, wise Odin was also a shaman—a sorcerer, a healer, a seeker after esoteric knowledge. He once traded an eye in return for a drink from the Well of Wisdom. On another occasion, he hanged himself from the great ash tree Yggdrasil, which stretched through the Norse universe from heaven to hell. Twisting from its branches for nine days, he gazed entranced into Niflheim, the Norse netherworld, and thus learned the art of writing with runes. Some legends say he gave his life for this knowledge, only to be reborn the wisest of all creatures.

Ritual death and rebirth is said to be the fate of all shamans in ancient times and among primitive cultures today. Acting as a link between this world and the next, the tribal wise man must prove his special status by going where no ordinary mortal may go: He must visit the land of the dead and return. Only after this ordeal will he be imbued with supposedly superhuman abilities, such as healing the sick, predicting the future, controlling the weather, ensuring successful hunts, and leading the dead to their rightful resting places in the beyond.

Possessors of these coveted mystical powers are said to have a special calling from the spirits, usually heralded by an illness, a trance, or an erratic change in behavior. Tribespeople view these signs as spirit messages and arrange for the initiate to undergo a ritual death. As part of this ceremony—during which the initiate may wear a mask, such as the Inuit one at right—the neophyte's spirit is said to embark on the first of many sojourns to the after-realm.

In most shamanistic cultures, there are three great domains of the dead—an underworld deep within the earth, a shallow realm just beneath the land's surface, and the sky. Peace and prosperity supposedly abound in the sky and the deep underworld; in the shallow realm, however, despair and famine reign. The prospective shaman is believed to travel between these worlds and that of the living by scaling a cosmic axis or "tree of life," a common symbol in many religions. At the tree's roots lies the underworld; at its base is the shallow realm; its branches touch the sky.

Wandering through this spirit world, the initiate may encounter monsters, along with the souls of many animals, dead shamans, and relatives, all of whom will impart divine secrets. He will also be confronted by spirits that he must battle. The spirits are both the shaman's bane and his salvation: They may attack and devour him or infect him with disease, "killing" him in order to restore his life in enhanced form. It is essential that the neophyte die, since it is from this ultimate experience that he gains his special power. Thus during the ceremony, which may last for several days, the initiate neither eats nor drinks; he lies still, scarcely breathing, usually in a solitary place.

After leaving him "dead" for a time, the spirits are said to return to reanimate his soul and impart all the remaining wisdom of the underworld. At the lesson's end, soul and body are reunited, and the resurrected fledgling shaman returns to the tribe. He will usually study with an older shaman for a time, even while exercising his new powers as healer, spiritual guide, and guardian of souls.

tions hinge on this threshold issue of the soul's existence: Is there life after death? And if there is not, how can human life have any value or meaning or moral purpose? Are we, for all our passions and striving, ultimately insignificant, not even ripples in an eternal tidal roll of cosmic indifference? Do our minds have no other fate than extinction and our bodies none other than corruption? Given the need to believe otherwise, it is no wonder that the idea of the soul has been a millenniums-long human obsession. There must be the hope, at least, that some essential part of the self will survive, carrying into an unknown after-realm all that it has learned and felt and remembered.

The search for the soul has led many to extreme conclusions—some inspired, some ridiculous—not only about if it is and what it is, but even where it is and how much of it there might be. One school of thought, now widely discredited, contends that the soul must reside in the pineal gland, a cone-shaped portion of the human brain whose functions are as yet indeterminate. Other researchers—literal-minded scientists—decided after elaborate experimentation that wherever it lurks in life, the soul must exist, for at death there is an infinitesimal but measurable weight loss representing its departure from the body.

Canny old James Kidd seemed to hope that the truth might turn out to be just that precise and quantifiable, that the soul was some substantial thing to be weighed and measured and even photographed. More literate people, familiar with all the subtle turns and nuances that have characterized the long and haunted intellectual journey toward the soul, might have doubted it.

Certainly, it was with some trepidation that Judge Robert Myers of the Superior Court of Maricopa County in Phoenix took on the case. A very literate man himself, Myers concluded long before the trial got underway that it would be like no other he had ever presided over. Quiet and scholarly, the judge found his life wrenched askew when news of James Kidd's staggering bequest became public. He was besieged and nearly overwhelmed by letters and phone calls as the pending proceedings took on the frenzied air of a supermarket sweepstakes. Dozens of would-be claimants sounded off, believing that they had only to provide a working definition of the soul to qualify for the grand prize—now worth more than $200,000. Through it all, Myers tried to maintain his good humor and sense of perspective. Surveying more than 4,000 letters that had poured in from twenty-six different countries, he offered the comment that his stamp collection, at least, would surely benefit from Kidd's generosity. But even Myers's forbearance seemed to wear a little thin when an especially persistent telephone caller, identifying himself as the evangelist Saint Mark, demanded a share of the money. "From which cloud was he calling?" wondered the judge.

The first order of earthly business, before the trial could begin, was to determine whether the scrawled document Geraldine Swift had uncovered was in fact James Kidd's valid last will and testament. An entire year passed before Myers could dispose of that matter and accept the will for probate, and it was another two years before the trial actually got started. On June 6, 1967, the judge brought down his gavel to begin the work of resolving the thorny central issues of the case: How and to whom was the money to be awarded? Who was best equipped to solve, or attempt to solve, the mystery of the soul?

he chambers of the Superior Court of Maricopa County seemed an unlikely place in which to attack the riddle. The stark, walnut-paneled courtroom appeared in every way better suited to prosecuting traffic violators than to abstruse philosophizing. Indeed, if any cosmic import were to be found in the trial site, it came from the city itself—Phoenix, the metropolis named after the legendary bird that is the very symbol of immortality. The creature is said to periodically consume itself in blazing fire, only to rise from the ashes renewed in life and spirit. With this oddly fitting emblem serving as his metaphorical backdrop, Judge Myers got to work. He knew the trial would be time consuming and con-

The Flight of Souls

"If he was a bad Indian, a hawk will catch the bird and eat it up, body, feathers, and all," a Kelta Indian proverb begins, "but if he was a good Indian, the soulbird will reach the spirit-land."

The image of the soul as a bird pervades the lore of numerous cultures and religions, from Paleolithic times to the present. As early humans pondered the idea of a surviving human essence and a life after death, they no doubt considered just how the spirit traveled from the body to its place in eternity. Perhaps the birds' ability to fly seemed a metaphor for transcending earthbound things, thus earning the winged creatures exalted status as bearers of souls.

The first people to use bird imagery for the soul's flight were probably tribes of the Old Stone Age. A cave painting in Lascaux, France, dating from 15,000 BC, shows a bison standing over a hunter it has killed. A bird sits on a nearby pole.

A 440 BC Greek vase painting illustrates the accidental slaying of Procris by her husband, Cephalus. As she dies, her soul, in the guise of a bird, flutters skyward.

Some scholars believe the bird represents the hunter's departed soul.

Among early civilizations, Egypt used the bird as an emblem for the soul. The hieroglyphic symbol of the ba, one of several entities the Egyptians equated with the soul, was a human-headed bird. The ba was believed to provide mobility for the person in the afterlife and to bring nourishment to the mummy to sustain it. Generally inactive during life, the ba was considered essential in the after-realm.

In other societies, birds were often thought to lead souls to paradise. In Syria, for instance, the eagle was said to perform this function, a belief also held by the early Romans, who released an eagle at an emperor's funeral pyre so the bird might carry the dead monarch's soul to the realm of the gods.

The eagle, along with the dove and the peacock, also was seen as a symbol of the soul. In both Judaism and Christianity, the eagle still stands for the hope of eternal life, and the dove is a symbol of the spirit of God. As for the peacock, Christians, noting how the bird shed its vivid feathers only to once again become sheathed in splendor, adopted the bird as a symbol of resurrection.

A symbol of immortality for Christians, the peacock, shown here in a detail from an Iranian manuscript of the 1600s, has been sacred for many peoples. In India, it was held to have curative powers; both Muslims and Hindus thought that it warded off evil.

The ba of Inherka, a master builder of Egyptian tombs, is depicted as a human-headed bird in this detail from a mural in his own Twentieth-Dynasty burial chamber. The ba was said to take various forms in the day to serve the deceased, returning to the tomb at night.

voluted. He could not have known that it would be one of the longest in Arizona history.

In all, 133 petitioners appeared before the packed courtroom to stake their claims. Many were easily dismissed: a woman who wanted a share of the pie to buy a new set of false teeth, a man who claimed that visitors from outer space had confided the secret of the soul to him, a woman who reported that the spirit form of Kidd himself had materialized in her bedroom. The prospector, she claimed, had decided to come along with her to the courtroom to share his thoughts on the trial.

If the ghostly Kidd was indeed present, he was probably nonplussed by the horde of purported relatives who appeared in pursuit of his estate. Although the miner had stated that he never married, a New York woman presented herself to the court as his widow and demanded her rightful share of his fortune. In addition, two elderly Canadians came forth to claim Kidd as their long-lost brother, and a pair of Wisconsin sisters professed to be his daughters. And there were oddities even more intriguing than the spirit summoners and the proliferating kinfolk: At the height of the courtroom drama, Judge Myers received a brief typewritten letter, whose writer revealed himself to be highly amused by the squabbling and scrambling over the money but expressed the hope that the funds would in time find their way into worthy hands. The letter was signed: "Quite Alive, James Kidd." The true identity of the author of this communique was never determined.

Despite all distractions, Judge Myers steered the proceedings past the obvious crackpots with quiet perseverance and began to consider testimony from some of the world's most prominent psychical researchers. These included Professor Gardner Murphy, president of the American Society for Psychical Research; William G. Roll, who had been an associate of Joseph B. Rhine at Duke University's parapsychology laboratory; and Ian Stevenson and J. Gaither Pratt, representing the Psychical Research Foundation, another well-established institution in the field of paranormal research. These men had devoted years to the study of purported psychic phenomena, including the survival question, and felt themselves to be best suited to comply with James Kidd's wishes.

A statement issued by the New York-based Parapsychology Foundation, yet another well-known and well-respected entry in the field, attempted to give shape to the question before the court: "The words 'human soul,' " it ran, "mean that part of that element (if any, whether tangible or intangible) of the psycho-physical organisms known as human beings, that survives death and continues in existence in some form or another after death with some conscious memory or tie to its past life." No further definition, the parapsychologists admitted, was truly possible in light of humanity's current knowledge: "If we knew what the soul was," the statement read, "scientific research would already have established its existence and general nature." Even so, the experts in the field of the paranormal firmly believed that their research might yet stumble upon some answers. "Presumably," the foundation's statement concluded, "Archimedes had nothing in mind but his bath when he suddenly discovered specific gravity."

lthough Judge Myers had allotted only eighteen days, the soul trial hearings stretched out over three months, running all through the hot Arizona summer of 1967. Several times over the course of the trial, the judge emphasized that the court's job was not to determine the nature of the human soul, but to decide which, if any, of the petitioners could best carry out the assignment mandated by James Kidd's will. But, unfortunately for the horde of people packed into the sweltering courtroom, the legal matter could scarcely be decided without considering the broader philosophical one. Even in the later stages of the trial, a number of hopeful litigants continued to try to impress the judge with outlandish and even otherworldly documentation. One petitioner produced a blurry spirit photo-graph that showed, he claimed, the very soul of James Kidd. Another ambitious claimant lectured the court at length on the difference between the human mind and brain, using a television set to represent the former and a can of spaghetti to illustrate the latter.

In this company, Gardner Murphy, who held degrees in psychology from both Harvard and Yale, proved refreshingly down to earth. As president of the ASPR, Murphy had made a long study of the phenomenon of crisis apparitions, or spirit manifestations associated with times of death or extreme personal peril. The psychologist described for the court deathbed accounts of the afterlife as reported by attending physicians and nurses, along with descriptions of purported out-of-body experiences and of physical events, such as the sudden stopping of clocks, that coincided with times of death.

Questioned as to how a link between such manifestations and the departure of the human soul might be established, Murphy was deliberately cautious. Sensors might be employed to detect changes in air pressure in rooms thought to shelter spirits, he speculated, and sound equipment and cameras might also produce registrable effects. Judge Myers pressed the matter further, pointedly asking whether the ASPR would, if awarded the Kidd money, be able to secure concrete evidence that a soul survives death. Murphy remained prudently conservative. "No," he said, "proof is much too strong a word."

For Judge Myers, this element of uncertainty only deepened his quandary. Three months of nonstop testimony had done little to clarify matters. Although he had disqualified Kidd's supposed heirs and ruled against those claims that took a theological rather than a scientific view, the judge found himself only slightly closer to a verdict. The conflict lay between two opposing groups of claimants: the parapsychology organizations, which believed that Kidd's wishes could be met through studying the possibility of human survival of death; and the more traditional scientific establishments, such as Phoenix's Barrow Neurological Institute. The institute, which had made no particular promises about how the money would be used toward the specific end of finding the soul, was dedicated to the study of the nervous system and life processes.

On October 20, 1967, following a lengthy period of deliberation, Judge Myers finally reached his decision. James Kidd, Myers announced, had intended that "his estate be used for the purpose of research which may lead to some scientific proof of a soul of the individual human which leaves the body at death. . . . Such research can best be done in the combined fields of medical science, psychiatry and psychology, and can best be performed and carried on by the Barrow Neurological Institute of Phoenix, Arizona."

The verdict created a sensation among all who had participated in the trial. Although no one doubted that Myers had made what he believed to be the fairest possible judgment, several of the parapsychology groups banded together to appeal the decision, leading to an additional five years of legal wrangling. In December 1972, the initial ruling was overturned on appeal by the Arizona Supreme Court, which awarded two-thirds of the money to the American Society for Psychical Research and the remaining third to the Psychical Research Foundation. At last, more than

Three Papua, New Guinea, natives breathe through tubes into effigies of their ancestors in an effort to reinvigorate the spirits of the dead. Like people of other cultures, the tribesmen view breath as the vehicle for soul.

19

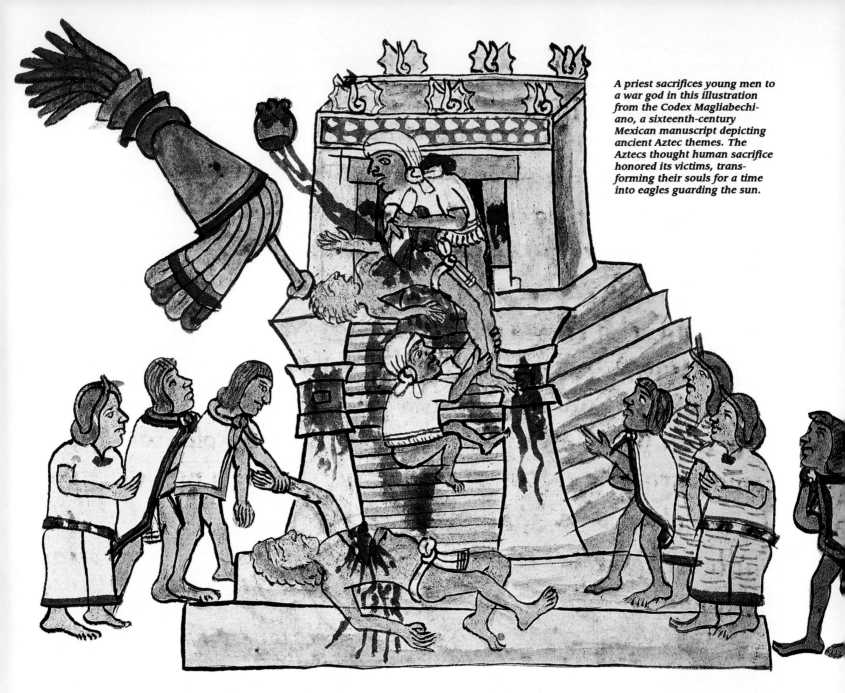

twenty years after the quiet-spoken prospector had disappeared into the Arizona desert, James Kidd's dream of a scientific search for the soul began in earnest.

For all the hoopla surrounding the Great Soul Trial, the seriousness and magnitude of the old miner's intent was never in question. After all, the riddle he wanted answered was a timeless one, and common to all humankind. "Since the dawn of history man has been preoccupied with death and the prospect of life beyond death," an attorney for the Parapsychology Foundation had stated at the height of the trial. "Most early tribes and civilizations believed in immortality. The majority of the billions of people now alive believe in a soul that survives death. It is something mankind has been interested in as far back as anybody can tell."

The foundation's attorney was quite correct. The majority of the world's earliest cultures nurtured a highly developed idea of the human soul and of its ability to persist beyond physical death. Frequently this survival was envisioned in terms of a world parallel and similar to the world of the living. Even primitive Neanderthal tribes evolved a custom of burying food and weapons along with their dead, apparently believing that the departed souls would have need of these things in another world. Sometimes the bodies of the dead were even painted with red ochre before burial, the sanguine hue signifying life and representing the possibility of physical resurrection.

As tribal cultures grew more advanced, so too did their concept of the soul. Many tribes believed—and some believe today—that the soul has a separate existence from

20

the body even during life. They came to associate disease with this crucial animating essence's having slipped away or been stolen. Illnesses thought to result from the absence of soul were brought before the tribal shaman, or miracle worker, whose job it was to recapture the soul and restore it to the sufferer's body. Only a shaman could perform these delicate cures, since only he had the power to detach his own essence from his material body and send it into the spirit world to reclaim the missing soul.

For the nineteenth-century-scholar Sir Edward Tylor, a professor of anthropology at Oxford, the beliefs of these primitive cultures held the key to the earliest stages of religion. In 1871, Tylor advanced his theory of "animism," which he defined as "the doctrine of souls and other spiritual beings in general." Early cultures, in Tylor's opinion, probably believed that everything in nature—including all natural entities such as trees, streams, and stars—were possessed of souls as well as bodies, souls that imparted life and movement. The soul, or anima, Tylor went on to state, "is a thin insubstantial image, in its nature a sort of vapour, film or shadow; the cause of life and thought in the individual it animates; independently possessing the personal consciousness and volition of its corporeal owner, past or present; capable of leaving the body far behind, to flash swiftly from place to place; mostly impalpable and invisible, yet also manifesting physical power."

Tylor's ideas did not pass unchallenged. A successor at Oxford criticized the animism theory on the grounds that it assumed primitive cultures grasped such relatively advanced concepts as "personal consciousness." Even so, Tylor's formulation exerted a powerful influence on future anthropological exploration of the nature and existence of the human soul. His work and that of others revealed that early humans had an abiding interest in identifying the precise location of the soul within the body. Blood, for example, was thought by many primitive peoples to be both the vehicle and substance of soul. In virtually every part of the world, in fact, blood has been been associated with soul by tribal cultures. The Greek historian Herodotus records that

the Scythians ritually drank the blood of their victims to absorb their courage and virtue. Certain peoples of West Africa and central Asia observed a bond of blood brotherhood by mixing a few drops of human blood with wine and drinking it down in order to signify a merging of essences and, by inference, undying fealty.

Sometimes these grim toasts were drunk from vessels fashioned from human skulls, for the head and brain also have a long association with the soul. Just as some primitive tribes believed that drinking blood was a way of absorbing a dead person's spiritual essence, others believed that the effect could be assured by feasting on the brain. Moreover, numerous rituals dating from prehistoric times tell of headhunting as well as the preservation and veneration of the human head as the sacred vessel of the human essence. In animal sacrifice, the head, considered to be the most valuable part of the body, was frequently preserved as an offering to the gods. And the same was sometimes true of human sacrifice. Beheading was an essential part of the ritual in which the Aztecs sacrificed their fellow mortals to the fertility goddess Teteoinnan and to Chicomecoatl-Xilonen, the goddess of young corn.

or some cultures, the soul dwelled not in the blood or head, but in breath or wind—a belief that probably stems from the cessation of breathing at the moment of death. Following a death in an Inuit community, mourners were known to plug their nostrils with deerskin or hay for several days to prevent their souls from following that of the deceased. Both Marquesans and New Caledonians used to hold the mouth and nose of dying people closed in an effort to keep them alive by keeping them ensouled. In Sulawesi, a sick person's nose was sometimes fastened with fish hooks in the hope that if his soul did manage to escape, it would be snagged on the hook and held fast. More influential cultures than these have also equated soul or life force with breath, a fact that is reflected in words they used to express aspects of

Aymara Indians of Puno, Peru, pour drink on the gravesites of their dead during the annual November 1 celebration known as the Day

of the Dead. The festival, called All Souls' Day in several other cultures, marks the hours when spirits supposedly return to earth.

pervasive preoccupation with the next life was rooted in the aesthetically minded Egyptians' love for earthly existence and their consequent horror of death, which seemed to bode a cessation of all joys and pleasures and the corruption of all beauty. They sought comfort in the belief that they had the means to achieve resurrection and to enjoy a happy and whole afterlife, with bodies and souls preserved intact.

In the Egyptian view of the self, an array of aspects, some physical and some incorporeal, made up every individual. Each of these was to a certain degree a constituent of the soul, playing a role not only in the welfare of the individual but also in the crucial preparation for the next world. Every person, the Egyptians believed, was composed of a natural body, a spiritual body, the heart, a double, the shadow, the casing of the body, and a body form. To complicate an already intricate equation, some of the aspects were subject to more than one interpretation. For example, a kind of soul the Egyptians referred to as the ka was sometimes regarded as a vitalizing force associated with breath and sometimes thought of as a double, an exact replica of the living person, which had been created at the moment of conception and existed throughout his or her lifetime. On the other hand, the ka could simply mean one's mental attributes or characteristic disposition—the soul as intelligence or as personality.

It was the ba, or heart-soul, however, that came nearer to the concept of the soul as a spirit that survives death. Often depicted in Egyptian art as a human-headed bird, the ba was believed to be a free-moving entity that separated from the body at death but remained nearby. Vital as these spiritual elements were, the perishable body, or *kbat,* was regarded as equally important to eternal well-being, which is why the Egyptians came to preserve the bodies of the dead so carefully against decay. Originally, they did not practice mummification; they simply buried or burned their

both: the Hebrew *nefesh* and *ruah,* the Greek *psyche* and *pneuma,* the Latin *anima* and *spiritus,* the Chinese *qi,* and the Sanskrit *prana.*

Not every society conceived of the soul as actually residing within the body. One tradition maintains that the soul is a physical double of its human host, existing in a separate but identical universe. Reflective surfaces such as mirrors, lakes, and streams were thought to capture the image of this spirit double, literally mirroring the soul. The ceremonial dress of the Mongolian shaman included nine hanging mirrors, thought to be gifts from the gods, the soul-reflecting powers of which could be used for healing. For the Papuans of New Guinea, a reflection glimpsed in a mirror could have fatal consequences, resulting from a loss of the "soul shadow." And in some other primitive cultures, it is believed that cameras, like mirrors, place the subject's soul in jeopardy by leeching away vital elements of the person's spirit.

Perhaps the most elaborate and multiform concept of the soul ever devised was that of the ancient Egyptians. Their beliefs evolved over thousands of years and resulted in a complex balancing of both physical and spiritual components. The surviving relics of their civilization, including the pyramids of the Giza plateau, the mummified remains of the Pharaohs, and the hieroglyphic record of their culture, attest to the fact that Egyptian society concerned itself with the afterlife to a degree previously unknown on earth. This

dead as other cultures had done before them. But as their belief in resurrection emerged, there came with it a need to preserve that which would be resurrected—the physical body itself. Undoubtedly, the Egyptians' fabled embalming techniques were not developed overnight, but once perfected, these rites became the center of their burial tradition and were practiced for centuries.

The mummification process combined clinical efficiency with ritual office: First the body was split open and all the internal organs except the heart were removed and stored in jars. It was thought that in the next world, the gods would weigh the heart against feathers to determine the balance of good and evil at the time of death. The balance was deemed a good indicator of how comfortably the individual might fare in the afterlife. With most of the organs removed, resins and perfumes were used to coat the chest cavity, which was then sewn up and soaked in a brine bath to prevent decomposition. After several weeks, the nose and mouth were padded with soft matter to replace perishable cartilage, and the brine-soaked corpse was carefully wrapped in linen body cloths.

These rites followed in accordance with the Egyptian *Book of the Dead,* a collection of funerary wisdom and customs that was gathered through the ages. The *Book of the Dead* played a significant role in the continuance of the burial tradition, with selections inscribed on the walls of tombs, on the sides of sarcophagi, or even on small scrolls of papyrus, which were tucked into the folds of the cloths enshrouding the corpse. These written extracts were meant to guide the departed into the next world, ensuring victory over enemies and ultimately enabling

the soul to reach the kingdom of Osiris, the god of the dead.

Of all the deities, Osiris, who had reigned as a king on earth and had been resurrected after death, loomed largest in the Egyptian belief in an afterlife. As ruler of Egypt, the legend goes, Osiris had redeemed his people from savagery and cannibalism by establishing a firm system of justice. Nevertheless, although he had achieved divine stature during his rule, Osiris suffered a brutal end at the hands of his own brother, the villainous Set. One night, in the midst of much drinking and high merriment, Set displayed a beautifully decorated wood and ivory coffer and boasted that he would present it as a gift to whatever man could fit himself

---

In temples clustered atop Mount Popa, an outcropping of rock located in upper Burma, natives gather once a year to worship a group of thirty-seven powerful spirits known as the Nats. During the course of the ceremony, dancers are supposedly ensouled by these spirits, who communicate their wishes through the whirling mediums.

within it. One by one each of the revelers stretched out in the bejeweled chest, but it fit none of them easily. When it came Osiris's turn to ease himself into the coffer, Set and his fellow conspirators rushed forward and nailed down the lid, sealing it shut with molten lead. The murderous crew then flung the coffer, with Osiris trapped inside of it, into the Nile River.

Eventually Osiris's body was recovered by his wife, the winged Isis, but Set soon regained possession of the corpse and hacked it into fourteen pieces, which he scattered across Egypt. With the help of the gods, Isis recovered her husband's limbs, swathed the re-formed body in bandages, and performed other necessary rites. Then, as she fanned the lifeless figure with her wings, Osiris arose from the dead to take his rightful place as the lord of eternity.

The story of Osiris held out the hope of resurrection to all Egyptians but only if the physical body remained pure and whole after death, allowing the proper germination of the soul. The Egyptians' horror of decay is rather graphically recorded in the *Book of the Dead* in the form of a plea from a mortal petitioning Osiris: "Let not my body become worms but deliver me as thou didst thyself. I pray thee, let me not fall into rottenness; . . . when the soul departeth (or perisheth) a man seeth corruption and the bones of his body rot and become wholly stinkingness, the members decay piecemeal, the bones crumble into a helpless mass, and the flesh becometh fetid liquid, and he becometh brother unto the decay which cometh upon him, and he turneth into multitudes of worms, and he becometh altogether worms, and an end is made of him."

Compared with the early Greeks' conception of the afterworld, however, the Egyptian images of fetid liquid and crumbling bones appear almost cheerful. For the Greeks, the prospect of death held only unrelieved torment. Although their philosophy would in time bear the seeds of modern thought about the soul, in its earliest stages Greek society offered only the bleakest view of what happened to the human essence in eternity.

Like the Egyptians, the early Greeks conceived of the soul as having multiple components. In the *Iliad,* the epic chronicle of the Trojan War, the Ionian poet Homer refers to two distinct types of human soul—a free soul, largely inactive during life, and a body-soul, which endowed the physical form with life and consciousness. The free soul represented a sort of impersonal life force, unrelated to intellect or emotion, rather than a unified entity with an independent existence. Thinking and feeling were the province of the body-soul, a concept that encompassed a number of components. One facet was the *thumos,* frequently mentioned in the *Iliad* as being the seat of human emotion. The thumos appeared to reside in the area of the human diaphragm, or *phrenes.* Thus, when Homer told of a warrior withdrawing his spear from a fallen enemy, the dead soldier's phrenes was said to prolapse because the thumos had departed from the body.

In the Homeric view, the physical body was as essential to the personality as the spirit was. With the advent of death, and the severing of the link between the body and spirit, the life force, or free soul, escaped and the body itself became "senseless earth," or dust. All that remained then was the eidolon, or image of the deceased, which was helpless without the body and was doomed to wander forever, lacking sensation of any kind. Only by cremation of the physical body was the eidolon freed to make the journey to Hades, the Greek underworld.

owever unpleasant the afterlife might be, the Greeks gave critical importance to cremation and the final releasing of the body image. Homer underscores the necessity of proper funeral rites toward the close of the *Iliad* after Achilles, the greatest of the Greek warriors, has killed his Trojan counterpart, Hector, son of King Priam of Troy. In a rage for Hector's slaying of Achilles' male lover, the Greek hero desecrates Hector's vanquished corpse, lashing it to his chariot and dragging it by the heels around the walls of Troy beneath the horrified

eyes of Hector's wife and parents. In a climactic scene of the epic masterpiece, Priam visits the camp of the hated Greeks and seeks out his arch-enemy to beg for the return of Hector's body. And fierce Achilles, remembering his own father and perhaps mindful that vengeance should not extend beyond death, relents and returns the corpse so that Priam might consign his son to a funeral pyre and thus free Hector's soul.

In contrast to the Egyptians and other earlier cultures, the Greeks made no offerings of food or other provisions for the journey to the afterlife. Instead, the body was hastened on its way as speedily as possible, and all personal effects were burned along with the corpse. This haste is surprising, however, considering the unremittingly grim view of Hades developed by the early Greeks. The underworld of Homeric times held no reward for a life of virtue or valor, only punishment for those who had offended the gods. For example, Sisyphus, an earthly king whose offenses included betraying certain secrets of the gods and killing strangers who sought his hospitality, was condemned to spend eternity in the backbreaking and futile task of rolling a huge boulder up a mountainside, only to see it roll back down time and again, and Tantalus, a son of Zeus who once served human flesh to the Olympians, was forced to endure endless hunger and thirst while fresh water and enticing fruit were eternally just beyond his reach.

The most vivid evocation of the torments of Hades comes in the *Odyssey,* Homer's tale of the Greek warrior Odysseus's long and turbulent voyage home to Ithaca after the end of the Trojan War. At one point in his journey, Odysseus travels to the border of the underworld, where "dreadful night has spread her mantle." There he digs a votive pit with his sword and fills it with the blood of slaughtered lambs. One by one, the dolorous shades of the dead appear and file past the pit. Those whom Odysseus permits to drink from the gory trench are briefly empowered by the blood to communicate with the living. Once-proud heroes straggle before Odysseus's eyes in pathetic review, reduced now to walking shadows bereft of life and spirit. Even the mighty Achilles appears only as a wan reflection of his former greatness.

Most painful of all, Odysseus beholds the shade of his own mother and finds that when he reaches out for her, her form slips through his embrace. Her words, after she has sipped at the pool of blood, express the agony of her underworld existence: "We no longer have sinews keeping bone and flesh together, but once the life force has departed from our white bones, all is consumed by the fierce heat of the blazing fire, and the soul slips away like a dream and flutters on the air."

Perhaps it was the very grimness, the unrelieved hopelessness of this conception of the afterlife that led subsequent Greek philosophers to introduce an element of redemption, along with a note of hope for the survival—with essential personality elements intact—of the individual soul. Writers after Homer would speak of the ability of the free soul to make journeys away from the living body, marking a shift in thought toward a more fully formed and conscious soul. This viewpoint is present in the ancient story of Hermotimos of Clazomenae, a city on the western coast of what is now Turkey. According to a tale that sounds much like modern accounts of out-of-body travel, Hermotimos's soul supposedly left his body and wandered freely for a number of years, traveling to different places and warning people of floods and other impending disasters. While his spirit ventured abroad, however, his body remained stiff and inert, as though dead, recovering only when the soul returned.

Herodotus, the Greek historian who is sometimes called the father of history, records the story of Aristeas of Proconnesus, who entered a cloth worker's shop and promptly fell to the ground, apparently dead. As news of the collapse spread, a witness reported having seen Aristeas outside of town at the very moment of his supposed death.

The Swathing of the Soul

An ancient Egyptian funerary ritual begins: "You have not gone away dead, you have gone away alive." Texts such as these reveal the Egyptian attitude toward life and death: Perhaps no other culture in history has been so preoccupied with life beyond the grave, so sure of its existence, or so intent on preparing for it. In this preparation, the body was just as important as the spirit, for the Egyptians thought that both bore the elements of soul.

Of the many relics, ruins, and rituals that survive to testify to this near obsession with the afterlife, the most telling are the mummies. In their exoticism, mummies have long fascinated cultures outside Egypt. Such was the mystique of the ancient, linen-shrouded corpses that in the sixteenth century they were even credited with magical healing powers. A powder derived from crushed mummies was said to cure a variety of disorders, ranging from cuts and bruises to upset stomachs. Demand for the powder became so great in Europe that there were scarcely enough imported mummies to fill the orders. By the nineteenth century, however, most of the mystery surrounding the mummies had dissipated, perhaps due in part to a new and popular upper-class parlor game—the unwrapping and dissecting of mummies.

What those gathered around the parlor table witnessed was the result of a process that took thousands of years to perfect. The Egyptians' first attempts at embalming began in the Fourth Dynasty, during the reign of Queen Hetepheres, and continued for almost three thousand years, until about AD 641. The practice of mummification—which essentially involved evisceration, curing with salt, and wrapping—reached its apex during the Twenty-First Dynasty, 1085-945 BC, and it was during this period that some of the finest mummies were created. Recently, radiologists from Brigham and Women's Hospital in Boston, in concert with that city's Museum of Fine Arts, conducted X-ray and CAT scans of a group of mummies dating from this period. They discovered such fragile structures as the optic nerve and the aorta still intact.

Eventually, the Egyptians' passion for preserving their dead began to wane. By the Roman period mummification had become more cosmetic than real. The covering and ornamentation of mummies—not the preservation of bodies—became an art unto itself. First, the corpse was wrapped in three layers of overlapping linen. Then cloth of varying colors was added to enhance the layering effect. Face panels displaying portraits of the deceased (right, center and bottom) took the place of linen and stucco masks of Osiris (right, top), and decorative details were included for persons of rank or wealth. Modern examinations confirm, however, that the bodies beneath these adornments were generally poorly preserved.

Early Egyptian mummification emphasized embalming the body. After this process, the face of the deceased was covered with a mask of Osiris made of stucco and linen, wood, or gold (top). By the Roman period (center and bottom), elaborate wrapping took precedence over embalming, and the mummies' faces began to be masked with portraits of the individuals.

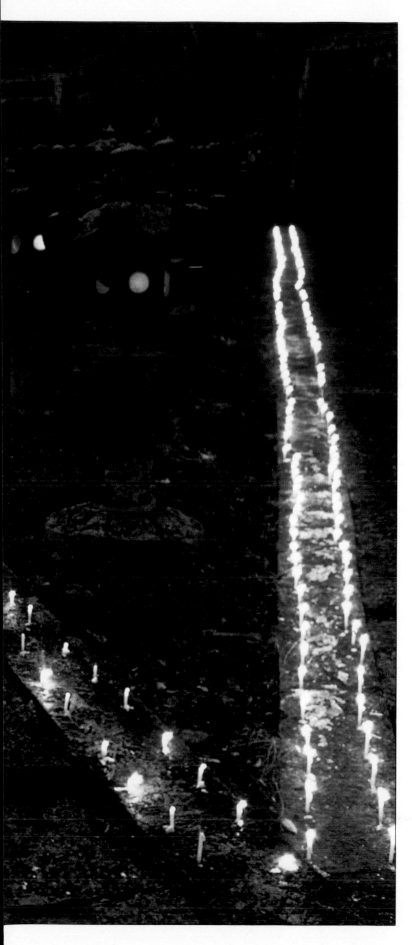

A Shinto priest stands on a path lit by hundreds of flickering candles, intended to guide the souls of the dead back to their graves in Japan's Mori cemetery. The tapers are lit at the end of the country's annual two-day Bon Festival, during which spirits of deceased relatives supposedly visit the living in order to offer advice and inspiration.

Stranger still, when relatives appeared to claim the body, no trace of it could be found. Six years later, Herodotus reports, Aristeas reappeared, body and soul apparently reunited, to compose a long poem chronicling a wondrous journey undertaken by his soul.

A later version of the tale describes the soul of Aristeas flying from his mouth in the form of a raven. Although the image recalls the beliefs of the primitive shamans, such tales of soul journeys—and the ability of a disembodied spirit to function independently of the constraints of the physical form—mark a significant advance in the concept of the soul. This notion of the soul freed from the body was a core belief of a cult devoted to the worship of Dionysus, the Greek god of wine.

Known as the personification of the sheer exhilaration produced by wine, Dionysus, according to one legend, once briefly assumed the throne of his father, Zeus, the supreme god of the ancient Greeks. After his ascent, he was attacked by jealous Titans, a race of gigantic gods who preceded Zeus and his Olympians as rulers of the universe. Changing shape in order to escape his foes, Dionysus took flight in the successive forms of a lion, a horse, and a serpent. When he transformed himself into a bull, however, the god was overcome by his enemies and, like Osiris before him, was brutally dismembered.

Early followers of Dionysus reenacted this gruesome scene by whipping themselves into a frenzy and tearing a live bull to pieces with their hands and teeth. These grisly rites, accompanied by loud music and the crashing of cymbals, were intended to propel the revelers into a state of ecstasy, a word literally meaning "outside the body" to the Greeks. Through this ecstasy, the cultists hoped to transcend their earthly bonds and allow the soul a temporary liberation from the body. Only in this way could the soul achieve a condition of *enthousiasmos,* meaning "inside the god," which the worshipers believed was a taste of what they might one day enjoy in eternity.

However violent and undisciplined, the Dionysian festivals afforded a lively alternative to the dreary view of the earlier Greeks. For the first time in the Greek tradition, the soul was perceived not only as having life and power but also as being touched by the divine. Even though the methods of the orgiastic maenads, Dionysus's female followers, met with widespread disapproval among the orthodox Greeks, the vision of the soul's communion with the superhuman proved to be an intoxicating notion, leading in time to the more temperate Orphic tradition.

 follower of Dionysus, the musician Orpheus endeavored to obtain the Dionysian liberation of the soul through nonorgiastic means, perhaps anticipating the fate that would one day befall him—being ripped apart by maddened worshipers during especially frenzied rites. Thus the tradition that bears Orpheus's name marks a move away from ecstatic rites, while retaining the idea of the soul's divinity. The followers of Orpheus turned the Dionysian method on its head, seeking ecstasy through abstinence and rites of purification, denying the senses rather than using them as vehicles for bliss. In the Orphic view, the soul was of divine origin but had been cast down to suffer imprisonment in human form. The reward or punishment awaiting it in the next life depended entirely on the degree of bodily purity attained on earth.

The philosopher Pythagoras devoted his life to refining and expanding the Orphic tradition. From his own mathematical and musical theories, Pythagoras evolved a concept of the soul as "a harmony of contrary elements united together in the body." Like the Orphists, Pythagoras believed in a divine soul requiring bodily purification. The philosopher took the notion a step further, however, speculating that following death the soul would seek rebirth in a new body, whether animal or human. This doctrine, known as transmigration, marks one of the earliest expressions of the soul as immortal, capable of undergoing cycles of reincarnation. It is scarcely surprising, given these beliefs, that Pythagoreans abstained from eating animal flesh. Pythago-

ras firmly held that even the lowliest animal body might retain a familiar soul. One story tells that the philosopher, chancing upon a man beating a dog, exclaimed, "Stop! Do not beat that dog! He is the soul of an old friend. I recognized his whine."

Such tales made Pythagoras a figure of some suspicion among his contemporaries, and many outlandish stories sprang up concerning both his eccentricities and his supposed supernatural powers. In time, the meeting place of his followers was set aflame, and Pythagorean beliefs were suppressed. History has been somewhat kinder to the great mathematician and mystic, although views continue to differ sharply as to the importance of Pythagoras's achievements and influence. The modern philosopher and mathematician Bertrand Russell described him as a combination of the unquestioned genius of physicist Albert Einstein and the dubious zealotry of Mary Baker Eddy, the American religious leader who, teaching that disease and death are "errors," founded Christian Science.

Whatever its merits, the philosophy of Pythagoras marked another turning point in Western civilization's concept of the soul. The theory of transmigration presupposed a new and different idea of a human essence that survives the death of the body intact. For many, the theories of Pythagoras held the germ of what is now the modern idea of the immortal soul.

It is unlikely that James Kidd, the lonely prospector from Arizona, felt any particular kinship with the likes of Osiris, Orpheus, or Pythagoras—if, in fact, he had ever heard of them. Nevertheless, the questions that haunted Kidd as he lay on the pump-house roof and stared up at the cold and faraway stars were little different from the concerns of the soul-healing shamans and soul-journeying Greeks. In his desire for "some scientific proof of a soul in the human body which leaves at death," the grizzled old miner joined all the generations that preceded him and all those that would follow, sharing a hope that the enduring enigma of the human soul might someday be made to yield up its secret.

Celebrations for the Soul

Many of the world's cultures display an odd split between faith and practice. On the one hand, people express the belief that the soul survives death to enjoy a glorious afterlife. On the other, they regard death with grief and mark it with mournful ritual. But there are places where no such contradiction exists. On two Indonesian islands, for instance, the inhabitants show their certainty of immortality by greeting death joyful, celebrating it as the soul's deliverance from its cumbersome earthly shell.

Natives of Bali and of Tana Toraja, on the island of Sulawesi, commemorate death with festive funeral rituals. The rites of the two cultures differ slightly, but both are rooted in animistic religions—faiths holding that all things possess a spirit as well as a material form and that the spirit, or soul, persists beyond the destruction of its temporal shelter.

Funeral rites in Bali and Tana Toraja are executed with great care, since the handling of the deceased is believed to determine the soul's future course. The splendor of each ceremony is an accolade to what the dead person did in life, and no expense is spared. Months and even years may be spent building spectacular biers and planning funeral games, processions, and feasts. The Balinese create intricate works of art, only to ultimately set them ablaze in tribute to the dead. The Toraja carve near life-size effigies of the deceased called *tau-tau (above)* and sacrifice worldly wealth to provide for departed souls in the afterworld.

A Fiery Tribute

For the Balinese, whose complex religion blends animism and ancestor worship with Hinduism, death is viewed as the happy first step on the path to reincarnation. But before the deceased may embrace what is hoped to be a better new existence, the physical body must be cremated. This final, critical act is believed to separate the soul from the body and purify it for the next life.

On Bali, cremation is a spectacular and expensive event, but it is not solely the province of the rich and the royal; the privileged are obligated to let commoners share in the ceremonies. Balinese of little means can bury their dead and then exhume them for inclusion in a wealthy person's funeral. Or they can bury them until enough money has been saved to mount a proper send-off independently.

The necessary rituals require weeks to complete and include erecting an enormous bamboo tower that is decorated with symbols of the cosmos. The tower's height and the number of its pagoda-like roofs, which represent the heavens, denote the caste of the deceased. At the tower's base, signifying the earth, is depicted the monstrous head of the god Bhoma, son of the earth and a guardian figure. Workers also construct wooden coffins for the dead. For nobility, the sarcophagus takes the shape of a bull, richly decorated with black velvet and gold leaf; for lesser Balinese, the coffins are carved to resemble various animals corresponding to the caste of the dead person.

Five days before the cremation takes place, a high priest visits the cemetery to awaken the souls of those previously interred to await the funeral ceremonies. The souls are bid to rise and rest in a magical tree while preliminary rites are performed to help speed them toward their new lives. On the day before the cremation, the bodily remains are exhumed, washed, and collected into bundles for consignment to the fire.

The remains of all destined for cremation are placed inside the tower. Amid a good deal of singing, dancing, and merriment, they are paraded to the cremation grounds, where they are transferred to the wooden coffins.

Special offerings are placed on the kindling, final prayers are said, and the fire is lit. Within minutes, the splendid tower and coffins are devoured by flames. The Balinese closely watch the fiery spectacle, for Hindus believe that if the smoke rises directly skyward, the deceased will reach a glorious realm.

At the cremation grounds, bearers of a bamboo tower position it near a ramp (right) that will be used to unload the body of a Balinese ruler. The corpse will be put in a sarcophagus for cremation.

Family members carry pictures of the dead and other offerings to the cremation grounds as part of the prescribed ritual. A failure to provide appropriate last rites for the deceased is believed to result in the soul's becoming a ghost and then tormenting its descendants on earth.

Bhoma, the guardian of temples, is enveloped in flames at the base of a cremation tower. The deity is usually depicted as a monster with wild eyes, massive tusks, and a wingspread extending to a width of twenty feet.

The glowing body of a dead Balinese ruler drops from the belly of a charred, bull-shaped sarcophagus. A large dragon bedecked with red velvet and gold leaf (foreground), denoting royalty, is provided to ferry the king's soul into the afterlife.

high in the mountains of Sulawesi, an orchid-shaped island that sits astride the equator. The isolated people of Tana Toraja practice rituals rooted in nearly 5,000 years of tradition. One of their most enduring and elaborate rites is the funeral ceremony, a celebration of dance, song, and feasts that lasts as long as seven days.

When a Toraja native dies, all family members are summoned to attend the funeral; to stay away would mean relinquishing one's membership in the clan. Burials are sometimes delayed for months or even years until all the kin can gather.

Until the funeral takes place, the deceased is not considered dead but merely sick. The corpse is wrapped and laid to bed in the family home; water and food are placed nearby. If the deceased was wealthy or of royal birth, a *tau-tau*, or wooden effigy, is carved to represent "the soul that is seen."

When the family has congregated, the complex series of funeral rituals begins. The body is taken from bed and repeatedly tossed into the air, a rite marking it as officially dead. Then a gong is sounded, and a buffalo is killed to proclaim the death.

The body is put into a coffin, which is placed into a *duba-duba*, a ceremonial bier. Its boatlike shape, like that of the houses of the Toraja, is said to honor the peoples' seafaring ancestors. Before a crowd lining the path, the bier is paraded through the village and rice fields. At times during the procession, those bearing the duba-duba begin to sway, run back and forth, and shake the bier to coax the soul from the body.

The bier is deposited in a ceremonial structure near a field where games, dances, and bullfights ensue. Gifts and animal sacrifices, thought to assure wealth and comfort in the afterworld, are lavished on the deceased. The most treasured offering is that of the water buffalo. The higher the

standing the deceased enjoyed in the community, the greater the number of buffaloes sacrificed at the funeral site—and, it is believed, the greater his or her status in the world beyond.

Following the festivities, the body and the tau-tau are carried to a cliffside burial place, where the remains are laid inside a family crypt and sealed behind a wooden

door. The tau-tau is placed at the crypt's entrance, positioned with its right palm outstretched to accept the rewards of the afterlife and its left palm held close to the body to ward off bad luck for future generations. Only then, it is believed, under the effigy's unwavering gaze, does the spirit of the dead Toraja begin its journey to Tondok Bombo, the realm of souls.

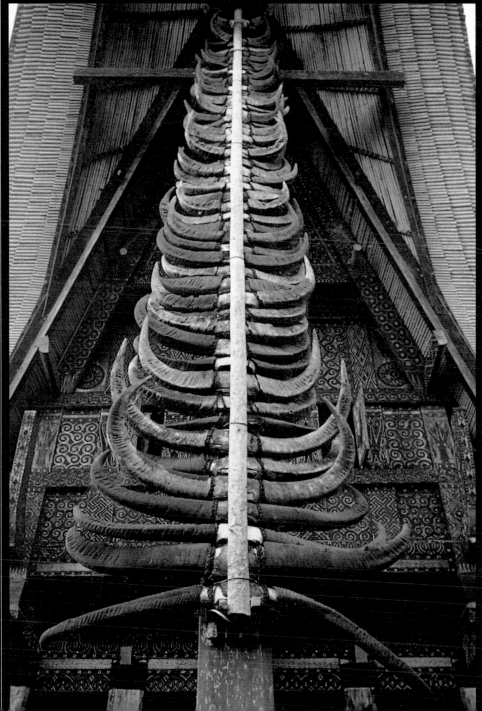

Amid festivity befitting a holiday parade, the ceremonial bier of a deceased Toraja nobleman makes its journey through the village. After the procession, the bier occupies a place of honor until burial.

The horns of sacrificed water buffaloes, remnants of previous funeral celebrations and symbols of high standing in the community, ornament the front part of one family's home in Tana Toraja.

Several generations of Toraja ancestors, depicted in this impressive gallery of carved

wooden effigies, flank family crypts that are recessed in the wall of a limestone cliff.

CHAPTER 2

Body and Soul: The Ghost in the Machine

or Socrates, it was the beginning of the end—or perhaps, as he himself might have noted, the end of the beginning. A month earlier, an Athenian court had sentenced this most renowned of thinkers to die by poison for his supposed "corruption of the young" and his "neglect of the gods." The charges were trumped up. Socrates' real offense was his habit of irking the Athenian establishment with frequent, trenchant criticism. The habit had earned him enemies both numerous and powerful. Still, he could easily have sidestepped punishment, either by fleeing Athens before the trial or by being more cooperative during the trial, or even, if necessary, by escaping after sentencing. But to avail himself of any of those options, though incurring no dishonor, would have implied guilt—an admission Socrates was not at all willing to make.

So now the fateful day was at hand. The year was 399 BC, and the balding and venerable philosopher was spending his final hours of it in the way he most enjoyed, in conversation with his friends and followers. If he found a jail cell an untoward setting for erudite discussion, he gave no sign of it, and if his friends seemed inclined to mourn, he did not. Among the disciples gathered that day was a young Athenian aristocrat named Plato, who was in the habit of writing down the master's words. It seemed a useful practice, since Socrates, though a relentless talker, never wrote anything down himself. Plato would collect the Socratic wisdom in a series of works called dialogues, and the influence of Socrates' conversations would thereby extend from ancient Athens to this very day.

Plato would also gather disciples of his own in a school called the Academy, so called because it met in an olive grove belonging to a man named Academe. Its most gifted student, one Aristotle by name, would come to reject much of the Academy's teaching and propose his own ideas in its place. In so doing, he would father a second great school of classical thought, and learned philosophers would argue for centuries to come whether he or Plato had been nearer the truth. But all these things were history yet unmade on that day when Socrates talked with his friends for the last time. The conversation was concerned not with history, but eternity—not with arguments, but with absolutes. Naturally enough on the day the master was to die, the discussion was of dying and the likelihood of an afterlife.

As Plato recounts in his dialogue the *Phaedo*, Socrates was himself convinced that death was just "the release of the soul from the chains of the body," and so he was prepared to drink the poison, hemlock, "rejoicing." But not all of his companions shared his optimism Cebes, for one, worried that upon death the soul, like air or smoke, would merely dissolve into nothingness. "Surely," said Cebes, voicing the fear that has bedeviled every age and every mortal, "it requires a great deal of argument and many proofs to show that when the man is dead his soul yet exists, and has any force or intelligence." The ensuing conversation consumed the remainder of Socrates' final day, and by the time the jailer arrived with the hemlock, the master had persuaded his disciples that the soul is imperishable and immortal.

If such thoughts were of immediate comfort to those at Socrates' side, they have nonetheless proved to be a mat-

ter of some philosophical dispute for later generations. Are we both earthly body and spiritual soul, as Socrates maintained, and does the immortal soul flee the mortal body at death for eternal life in another world? Or are we merely breath, as other philosophers have contended, and destined at death to be dispersed once and forever by the indifferent breeze? "This doubt there is about a man departed," says Naciketas in the Hindu Katha Upanishad, "some say: He is; some: He does not exist."

The search for the soul was at first the province of religion and was a matter of emotion and faith—which, for many, it remains today. Along the road, however, philosophers joined the quest, trying to reason their way toward determining the soul's existence, defining it, comprehending its fate. Many a profound thinker has pondered over the soul in the centuries since Socrates, and all manner of speculation has resulted.

Foremost among the ponderers was Plato himself, whose own thoughts became the bedrock of Western philosophy. Indeed, such is his influence that the British philosopher and mathematician Alfred North Whitehead observed that the whole of Western philosophy is only a series of footnotes to Plato. It was Plato who first postulated the so-called dualistic concept of mind and body—or soul and body. (He used the Greek word *psyche,* which can be translated either as mind or soul.) Dualism holds that each person consists of an incorporeal soul temporarily imprisoned in a corporeal body. To Plato the soul is "in the very likeness of the divine, and immortal, and intellectual, and uniform, and indissoluble, and unchangeable." The body, by comparison, is none of those things.

As part of that same theory, Plato contends that the soul exists in its own right, that it not only survives the body, but preexists it as well. Moreover, Plato declares that the soul, not the body, forms the real or true person, a claim that can only have mystified the average Greek in the Agora, who, when he thought of the soul at all, most likely thought of it as a puff of air or an invisible vapor or a pitiable shade in some grim and insubstantial nether world. After all, how could the soul be the true person when it was common knowledge that the true person was the flesh-and-blood person one could see, hear, touch, and smell?

 simple statement of the Platonic answer appears in the *Alcibiades I,* a dialogue that asks the questions, "What are we, and what is talking with what?" In the dialogue, Socrates reasons that the act of speaking uses words, just as a shoemaker uses tools. Always, however, the user and the thing being used are distinct entities, which implies that the person using his body has to exist apart from that body—or, as Socrates phrases it, "either man is nothing at all, or if something, he turns out to be nothing else than soul."

Plato's developed view is that soul, which constitutes the essence of humanity, is not a single entity. He argues for the existence of a three-part, or tripartite, soul. It comprises, in order of their importance, a rational element (reason) and two irrational elements (the "spirited" part and the bodily appetites). Although they make up a unit, each of these three components has its own objective: The rational element desires truth and wisdom; the spirited element expresses the emotional drives of honor, courage, pride, and ambition; and the bodily appetites seek gratification of their desires. Only rarely and in rare individuals are the three elements in harmony, producing a sense of inner peace and happiness, a state of well-being that Plato refers to as "the justice of the soul."

More often, the three elements are in direct conflict with one another, and in the *Phaedrus,* Plato uses the image of a man driving a chariot to depict the consequences of this intrasoul strife. Drawing the chariot are two horses, pulling in opposite directions, one horse responsive to the man's commands and symbolizing the emotions, the other uncontrollable and representing the bodily appetites. Forever wrestling with the reins is the charioteer himself, the embodiment of reason. In another dialogue, the *Republic,* Plato again depicts reason as a man, but this time the spirited element is symbolized by a lion and the bodily appetites by a many-headed dragon. Attaining that elusive justice of the soul is only possible if the man can convince the lion to help him keep the dragon in check.

If the emotions and bodily appetites are frequently unruly, the body itself, according to Plato, is a burden that is riveted to the soul by the nails of human pleasure and pain. Only death can relieve the soul of this encumbrance. Death, therefore, is to be welcomed as "a release and separation from the body" and not to be feared as some "sort of hobgoblin," as Cebes calls it in the *Phaedo.* In fact, the life of the philosopher is a "rehearsal for death" in the sense that the philosopher is continually seeking to release the soul from the body and its passions in order to achieve true knowledge of reality. "The true philosopher practices dying," Socrates says.

Those philosophers who listened to Plato could well afford to embrace dying, since Plato was confident about the soul's immortality. In fact, the soul and its endless pilgrimage occupy much of the *Phaedo.* In it, Plato shows Socrates striving to convince his students Cebes and Simmias of the immortality of an immaterial soul.

Although Cebes and Simmias want to share Socrates' faith in an eternal tomorrow, their disbelief continues until it is routed by the master's final argument. Socrates explains to his doubting listeners that every word, such as *beauty* or *equality* or *heat,* is linked to an abstract Idea, or

Reincarnation in the West

That the human soul survives death to be reembodied later is a belief most commonly associated with Eastern philosophy and religion. However, the ideas of reincarnation (rebirth in human form) and transmigration (encompassing the possibility of returning as a lower life form) have deep roots in Western civilization as well.

Plato's *Republic,* for instance, recounts the legend of the warrior Er, who returns to life several days after being killed in battle. During his time in the realm beyond, Er sees souls awaiting rebirth, souls that will themselves select the form of their next incarnation. Whether they choose well or foolishly, Er explains, depends on insights acquired during previous lives. Before returning to earth as humans or animals, the souls drink from the river Lethe—the waters of forgetfulness—to erase all memory of the past.

The notion of rebirth found its way into the thinking of several early Christian theologians, including Origen, an Egyptian from Alexandria, who taught that the soul experiences successive

lives until finally, enlightened and unblemished, it is fit to enter heaven.

Such views were condemned as blasphemy by Pope Anastasius in AD 400, and Origen's "monstrous doctrine" was declared anathema by the Second Council of Constantinople in 553. Nevertheless, a number of Christian sects clung to a belief in reincarnation. Particularly influential and long-lasting were the Cathars ("purified ones") of medieval France. Although they were frequently persecuted by the Catholic church for heresy, the Cathars lasted until the mid-thirteenth century, when many of their members were massacred during a Catholic siege of their fortress of Montségur in the French Pyrenees.

Western interest in the soul's rebirth revived in the mid-nineteenth century, at about the same time that Spiritualism—whose basic tenet was the soul's survival—flared across America and Europe. In fact, the word *reincarnation* was coined by the founder of a Spiritualist splinter group, the Frenchman Allan Kardec. Although mainstream Spir-

In this nineteenth-century painting by R. Spencer Stanhope, souls entering the river Lethe emerge naked on its other shore—stripped literally and figuratively of all vestiges of their former lives.

itualism took no special position on reincarnation, Kardec insisted that rebirths were necessary for the soul's evolution toward perfection.

Another nineteenth-century advocate for reembodiment was Helena Petrovna Blavatsky, whose Theosophical Society borrowed from Eastern ideas about reincarnation. These included karma, the notion that behavior in one life determines fate in the next.

Although the East remains the stronghold of belief in reincarnation, some Western parapsychologists study it. Notable is Dr. Ian Stevenson, a professor of psychiatry at the University of Virginia, who continues to document alleged cases of rebirth. Moreover, the idea of multiple past lives—explored under hypnosis as part of a process called past-life therapy—has become a standard New Age belief.

Form, that is both changeless and eternal. Thus the Form of Heat exists in the immutable realm of eternally true Forms, separate from the actuality of some object that is hot. Moreover, Socrates maintains, a Form is incompatible with its opposite; hence, the Form of Heat cannot coexist with the Form of Cold, and when confronted by heat, cold will either withdraw or perish.

Socrates next proposes that the soul, as the unseen force that renders the body alive, participates in the Form of Life. Life's opposite is, of course, Death; but since a Form never admits its opposite, Socrates reasons that the soul can never accept death. Instead, "when death attacks a man, the mortal portion of him may be supposed to die, but the immortal retires at the approach of death and is preserved safe and sound." The conclusion, as Socrates informs his now convinced listeners, is inescapable: "The soul is immortal and imperishable, and our souls will truly exist in another world."

Nevertheless, "the fact of being born," as the twentieth-century philosopher George Santayana points out, "is a poor augury of immortality," for if indeed we are born from nothingness, should not death only mark our return to the void? A similar thought haunted the Roman philosopher Lucretius, who, along with many others of his time—three centuries after Plato wrote—saw the nothingness before birth as a precursor to the annihilation of death. "When the body has been shattered by the mastering might of time," Lucretius wrote, "it naturally follows then that the whole nature of the soul is dissolved, like smoke, into the high air."

Plato, however, would have countered that the soul existed in a mortal body before birth and will surely exist again after its exile by death. In the *Phaedo,* Plato has Socrates explain that life and death, like cooling and heating, form a process that involves "a passage into and out of one another," or in modern parlance, reincarnation, or a transmigration of souls. Thus, according to Socrates, the living are generated from the dead and the dead from the living, and life on earth is only a way station on the soul's trackless journey to some higher realm of pure intelligence. In the *Meno,* Plato, again using Socrates as his mouthpiece, notes that priests and poets "say that the soul of man is immortal, and at one time has an end, which is termed dying, and at another time is born again, but is never destroyed." The moral, Socrates explains, is that a person should always live in perfect holiness lest his lack of virtue merit misfortune in a later life.

Another of Plato's dialogues, the *Timaeus,* tells the story of a man who failed to lead a virtuous life and was punished by being reincarnated as a woman—a dismal fate, so the Greeks believed, since women were considered inferior to men. Should the man fail a second time, he would be changed "into some brute who resembled him in the evil nature which he had acquired."

lato bolsters his argument for immortality and the prebirth existence of the soul by asserting that all learning is not really learning at all, but remembering: All our knowledge in this life was actually gathered in some previous one. The soul is immortal, Socrates asserts, "having been born again many times, and having seen all things that exist, whether in this world or in the world below." The argument expressed in the *Phaedo* and the *Meno* is that man has a knowledge of absolute truths and standards that the actual world could not have given him; therefore, this knowledge must have been gained in some former existence. As Socrates tells Simmias, "Our souls must also have existed without bodies before they were in the form of man, and must have had intelligence."

Plato's dualistic concept of the soul as a deathless entity tied from time to time to a mortal body, and the Platonic doctrine of learning as recollection, were adopted almost in their entirety by his most famous student, Aristotle—at least at first. Indeed, in an existing fragment of the young Aristotle's lost dialogue, the *Eudemus,* he not only describes the

A Roman mosaic from the first century AD pays homage to Plato's Academy, which opened in Athens in about 385 BC. Plato, pointing toward a sphere at his feet, taught his disciples mathematics and the natural sciences, but philosophy—including arguments for an immortal soul—was the centerpiece of study.

The Neoplatonic Soul

In the third century AD, ideas based on Platonic concepts coalesced into a new philosophy called Neoplatonism. At its center was the brilliant Egyptian Plotinus, who turned Plato's notion of two worlds—one transcendent and one material—into a new cosmic architecture. The core of Plotinus's vision is the One, or the Good. So remote is the One in its perfection that nothing can be predicated upon it: It is not possible even to say "the One is" without presuming what cannot be known. Says Plotinus: It is "beyond being." Beneath the One are two realms, intellect and soul. The sphere of the intellect is beyond time, changeless and eternal. Its hallmark is intuitive understanding—the direct apprehension of reality. Below the intellect, the soul is a realm of reasoning, of restless questing from premises toward conclusions in search of reality. Soul forms and animates the material world; every material thing shares in it.

A two-way mobility applies in Plotinus's cosmos. Intellect yearns upward toward the One but can reach down to the world of soul. Similarly, soul desires union with intellect but can extend down to the smallest particle of matter. The aim of the wise, Plotinus says, is union with the One, to be achieved by casting off worldly concerns and undertaking strict moral and intellectual discipline.

The last great pagan philosophy, Neoplatonism influenced both Christian and Muslim thought before fading in the sixth century BC. Although it died as a movement, its emphasis on invisible worlds helped shape the thinking of some modern mystics. Among them was the visionary eighteenth-century English poet and painter William Blake, who exalted the human imagination as the highest form of the soul. Blake set himself a "great task": "To open the Eternal Worlds, to open the immortal Eyes / Of Man inwards into the Worlds of Thought, into Eternity / Ever expanding in the Bosom of God, the Human Imagination."

The soul swoops down from heaven amid the flames of Judgment Day to embrace its former body in a William Blake engraving that illustrated Robert Blair's poem entitled "The Grave." Reflecting a Neoplatonist belief, Blake depicts the soul as feminine, regardless of the gender of the body.

soul as a separate substance, but characterizes its relationship to the body as an unnatural union. He compares it to the torture used by Tyrrhenian pirates in which live prisoners were lashed to corpses.

But while Aristotle's youthful views were tied to Plato's Academy, the bonds frayed. Aristotle gradually altered his theory of body and soul, adopting, in the beginning, a belief in the body as an instrument of the soul. The body is like a ship and the soul like its captain, or the body is like an object and the soul like the hand that manipulates it. Still later, he came to see the soul as the quickening force that animates a living body. By the time he died in 322 BC, Aristotle, whom the great Italian poet Dante would one day refer to as "the master of those who know," had abandoned virtually all of the Platonic metaphysics that he had once espoused as a young man.

The theories of the mature Aristotle are most apparent in his great treatise *De Anima,* or "Of the Soul," his attempt "to ascertain the nature and essence of soul" as the principle of life. "What is it?" Aristotle asks himself in the opening paragraphs. He answers by first defining what the soul is not, in the process refuting many theories popular at the time. The soul, says Aristotle, is not a fire, as the atomist Democritus believed, or air, as Diogenes and others claimed, or blood or water, as still others would have it. Likewise, the soul is not a harmony of substances, nor is it capable of movement, nor is it intermingled in the whole universe. Most important, the soul is not a separate entity.

What the soul is, according to Aristotle, is the animating form of a living body. "What has soul in it," writes Aristotle, "differs from what has not, in that the former displays life." In other words, the soul is that thing that determines, by its presence or absence, what is alive and what is not. By that standard, not just humans, but also plants and animals have souls, although none is as highly evolved as the human soul. Aristotle sees every living thing as consisting of formed matter—inchoate material that is given form by the soul. In other words, soul directs the realization of matter's potential. The soul is a sort of blueprint, the source of instructions that direct matter to achieve its purpose: The oak tree is the purpose that the matter of the acorn serves.

Moreover, since each living thing is a unity of body and soul, of matter and form, the soul is inseparable from its body, and the death of the body brings with it the death of the soul. Contrary to what Plato had suggested to his adherents, Aristotle assured his followers that there is no eternal life for individual human souls and no reincarnation. The only immortal soul is that of the Unmoved Mover of Aristotle's *Metaphysics.* The Unmoved Mover is the eternal first cause of the ceaseless change and motion of the universe. God is the name Aristotle gives to the Unmoved Mover, whose only activity is contemplating his own thought.

In breaking with the Platonic dualistic concept of the soul, the mature Aristotle became the philosophical founding father of the monistic traditions, the schools of thought that see body and soul as a unit rather than as two distinct and separate substances.

Over the ensuing centuries, generations of scholars and theologians would side with either monism or dualism. Some, such as Saint Augustine, for whom the soul was a

"rider" on the body, opted for Plato's concept of body and soul as discrete entities. Others, including the twelfth-century Moorish philosopher Averroës, favored Aristotle's vision of body and soul as a single substance. Still others steered a middle course. Foremost in this contingent was Saint Thomas Aquinas, who sustained the Catholic church's hold on the human soul by inserting his doctrine of resurrection—the reviving of the body and the soul to face God's decreed salvation or damnation—between Plato's disembodied soul and Aristotle's soul "united to the body as form to matter."

By the seventeenth century, however, science was challenging the Church's view of the universe. Against the comfortable notion of the Earth as the center of all creation, Copernicus had already placed the Earth in its rightful orbit around the Sun. And Galileo, at the risk of being branded a heretic, had seconded the Copernican theory. Isaac Newton was waiting in the wings to give the universe a mechanistic and materialistic order, and the stage was set for a French lawyer's son who would reject the theories of his philosophical predecessors, dedicate himself to "the destruction of all my former opinions," and upend Western philosophy with three Latin words: *Cogito, ergo sum.*

René Descartes's revelation "I think, therefore I am," formed what he intended as a point on which to balance a philosophical fulcrum and shift the world's view of itself. Very nearly that momentous in the intellectual scheme of things, the cogito was the culmination of another event of enormous significance—if only, in the beginning, to Descartes himself. Its importance is only hinted at in his diary: "10 November 1619: I was filled with enthusiasm, discovered the foundations of a marvelous science and at the same time my vocation was revealed to me."

The twenty-three-year-old soldier and would-be philosopher had spent most of that cold November day as he had spent many previous ones: alone in his heated room in Ulm, Germany, mentally examining the knowledge he had accumulated during his young life, rifling

The Grim Reaper, probably denoting the arrival of a plague, claims victims in this miniature from a 1503 French manuscript. Sudden death, a familiar event in the disease-ridden Middle Ages, was especially terrifying because the soul's fate was thought to hinge on one's spiritual state at the moment of death.

A revitalized body climbs from its grave in this detail from Luca Signorelli's early sixteenth-century fresco entitled The Resurrection of the Flesh. *Followers of Christianity, Islam, and Zoroastrianism all believe that on a final judgment day those who have died will rise from the earth and bodies and souls will be reunited.*

the contents of his brain in an effort to find the thread he believed would bind all the sciences. That night an exhausted Descartes surrendered to sleep, only to have his life redirected by complicated and symbol-fraught dreams—dreams that revealed, he thought, a simple, unified science connecting philosophy and all existing sciences in one mathematical, systematic totality.

Another man might have brushed off the dreams as an extended nightmare, but Descartes saw the hand of God in his "illumination." Later, pondering the possible meanings of the phantoms, whirlwinds, and peals of thunder that had visited him in the night, he became convinced that his mission in life was to seek the unity of all truth by building a new science on the ruins of the old.

Aglow with the fervor of the newly enlightened, Descartes not long afterward confided to a notebook that he was ready to "go forward in this theater of the world where until now I have only been a spectator." Despite this expansive pronouncement, he would spend the next eighteen years living a solitary existence, refining the tenets of his "marvelous science." Throughout that period, he lived, in the words of the twentieth-century French philosopher Étienne-Henry Gilson, "by thought alone for thought alone," helped in no small measure by an inheritance that freed him from financial worry and bought him the leisure to spend half of every day in bed. So consuming was Descartes's passion for truth that he forswore even marriage in the belief that "no beauty is comparable to the beauty of truth."

Descartes's single-mindedness was finally rewarded in 1637 when he wrote his renowned *Discourse on Method*. In this and later works, he spells out the mind-over-matter theory that has come to be known as Cartesian dualism. A modern offshoot of Platonic dualism, Cartesian dualism claims that reality consists of two kinds of substances, mental and physical. Mental, spiritual substance has as its principal attribute thinking. Minds have no spatial extension, are not measurable, are not in motion, do not move on impact. Physical substance, on the other hand, is defined by being extended in space and measurable by geometry. Its motion is mechanical and the result of impact. But physical substance has no mental, spiritual, or conscious attributes. The thorny problem of the Cartesian construct, as critics subsequently would point out, is how to account for the interaction of mind and body, now defined not only as separate entities, but as wholly antithetical realities.

The "method" cited in the book's title is a system of thinking by doubting—approaching all premises from a stance of extreme skepticism, accepting only the one truth Descartes finds unassailable—the cogito—and reasoning from that toward more com-

As an aspect of his theory of mind-body dualism, the seventeenth-century French philosopher René Descartes equated the mind, or consciousness, with the human soul.

plex conclusions. He conceives of this discipline as a wrecking bar with which to pull down the houses of science and philosophy and a tool with which to rebuild them according to his own specifications. Accordingly, he wastes little time in the *Discourse* in putting his method to work, first by dismantling all of his own prior knowledge, so "that everything that ever entered into my mind was no more true than the illusions of my dreams."

But was it? Certainly, as Descartes explains, he can mentally erase his own body, the world, and his immediate surroundings. But try as he might, he cannot doubt his own existence because the conscious act of doubting requires thinking, and thinking entails existence as a thinking substance. The truth, writes the suddenly enlightened Descartes, is self-evident: *Cogito, ergo sum.* "I think, therefore I am." This truth is undeniable as well as inescapable, since to deny it also requires thinking, and to think is to exist.

The cogito became the cornerstone for the unified science Descartes intended to build—both cornerstone and key, in fact, for from that one principle Descartes deduces that he is a substance whose entire nature is to think, and one whose existence is independent of his body and his surroundings. Accordingly, "this 'me,' " as Descartes describes himself, "that is to say, the soul by which I am what I am, is

entirely distinct from body . . . and even if body were not, the soul would not cease to be what it is."

That soul, Descartes believes, is not in any way derived from the power of matter. Rather, it is expressly created and lodged in the body, which is itself only a "machine." Moreover, although the soul shares the appetites and sensations of the body, it remains independent of its temporary domicile and does not die with it. Insofar as Descartes can learn, there is nothing that can destroy the soul, thus it must be immortal.

The *Discourse* returns to the subject of immortality, but not before pausing to examine in light of the cogito the next links in what Descartes calls his "chain of truths": the existence of God and of nature in the light of the cogito. According to Descartes's method of thinking by doubting, to doubt that God exists is to have no hypothesis to explain "my idea of God as a being with all perfections." God must exist, Descartes reasons, and it is God, "a perfect and infinite Being," who gave order to the chaos that had been the universe, setting it in motion before abandoning it to the laws of mechanics. The same God then "formed the body of a man just like our own," Descartes says, "and created a rational soul and joined it to the body."

Four years after publishing the *Discourse,* Descartes elaborated on the nature of the soul and the existence of God in his philosophical masterpiece, *Meditations on the First Philosophy.* As he did in the *Discourse,* the author relies here on his system for unearthing truth, first by surrendering wholly to doubt, denying the body and its senses and any fact or sensation that memory might ever dredge up. But in the *Meditations,* Descartes pushes his theory of thinking by doubting to its limits, casting God as an evil genius

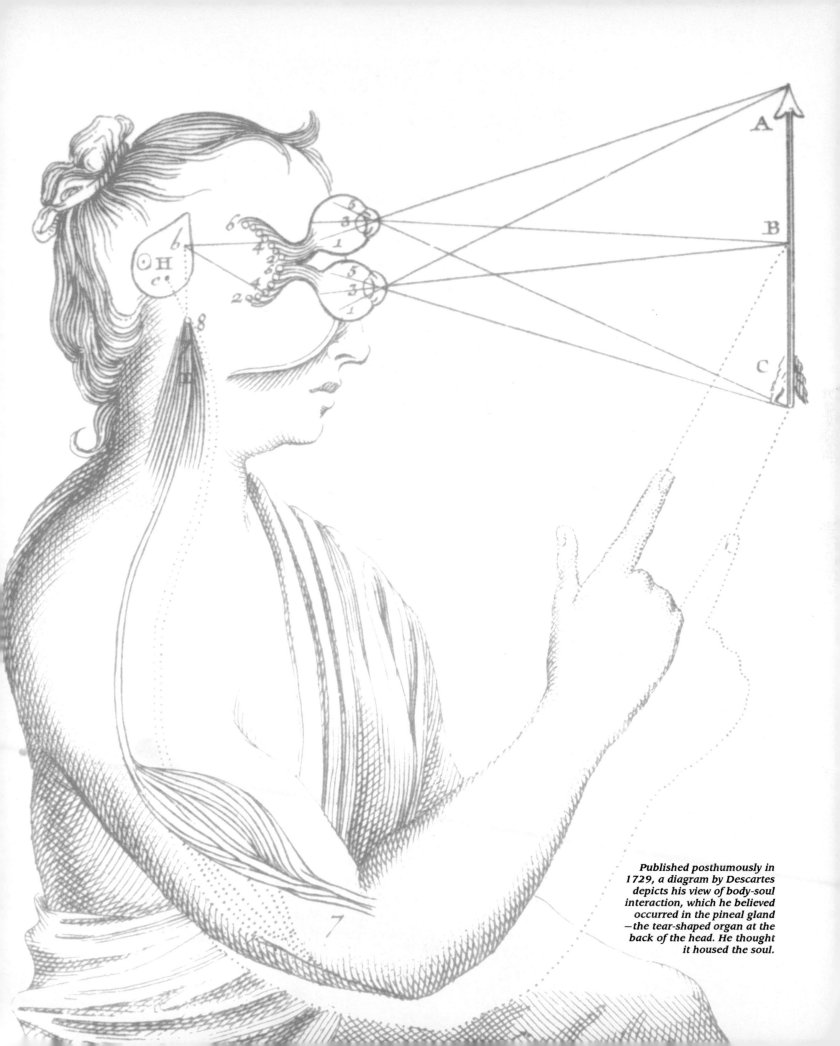

Published posthumously in 1729, a diagram by Descartes depicts his view of body-soul interaction, which he believed occurred in the pineal gland —the tear-shaped organ at the back of the head. He thought it housed the soul.

The Quest for Spiritual Gold

Praised by some as a noble pursuit and ridiculed by others as a false science, the ancient art of alchemy—which attempts to transform base metals into gold—has long tantalized the human imagination. Developed in Egypt, probably during the first century AD, alchemy was practiced by the Chinese, Indians, Arabs, and Greeks. Little knowledge of their methods has survived from antiquity, but many medieval alchemic texts still exist. From these obscure pages, some modern-day thinkers have determined that true alchemy was as much a quest for spiritual riches as material ones.

The alchemist's goal on the material plane was to create the philosophers' stone, the elusive substance said to perfect lowly metals by turning them into pure gold. Greatly simplified, this mystical process—called the great work—comprised three stages, the completion of each signaled by a particular color. First, the alchemist heated a material called the first matter—probably a blend of salt, mercury, and sulfur—until it dissolved into liquid and turned black with decay. Then, again under the influence of heat, the liquid was desiccated and the matter reborn, but this time colored white. In the third and final stage, if the alchemist was successful, the material would recombine and emerge brilliant red, the hue denoting the coveted philosophers' stone.

The chemical stages of the great work were assumed to be paralleled by spiritual changes in the alchemist himself. As the legendary sixteenth-century physician Paracelsus put it, the alchemist was "ripened" by his art, just as lesser metals were ripened into gold. The act of breaking down the first matter corresponded to the alchemist's mercilessly examining his innermost soul until it too lay rotted and dead. From this ruin, the spirit supposedly arose anew, and the alchemist toiled to create the spiritual equivalent of the philosophers' stone—a pure and immortal soul.

Medieval alchemists recorded the details of their craft in highly symbolic and abstruse texts and illustrations that defied interpretation by those outside the art. Although skeptics claimed the secrecy was merely a veil for the emptiness of alchemy's promises, it probably also served the practical purpose of averting persecution for heresy. The Church would not have looked kindly on the notion that one's own efforts could perfect the soul and thus free it from earthly bondage. Believers also argued that the writings were deliberately oblique to ensure that the treasured knowledge did not fall into unworthy hands.

Almost from the first, alchemy developed along two paths—one emphasizing the sort of practical experimentation that would ultimately lead to modern chemistry, the other more mystically inclined. By the eighteenth century, mystical, allegorical alchemy had become estranged from science and the respectability that science had once afforded. Yet mysticism would make it the survivor of the two strains. Most contemporary alchemists believe that the quest for gold and the pursuit of a pure soul go hand in hand but that the noble metal is merely a by-product of spiritual enlightenment. And many so-called New Agers have embraced the spiritual implications of alchemy, which to them symbolizes a way of life that exalts spiritual values over material goals.

An alembic, or distillation vial, encloses three birds in this detail from a sixteenth-century alchemic manuscript. The birds' colors symbolize the three stages in creating the philosophers' stone and in the alchemist's spiritual quest.

and "arch-deceiver" and mentally reshaping the heavens and earth into one vast deception.

But out of deception springs certainty, for in imagining himself deceived, Descartes, or some part of Descartes, is thinking, and if thinking, he must exist. Let God, if he be an arch-deceiver, "deceive me as much as he will," Descartes argues, for "he can never cause me to be nothing so long as I think that I am something." The fact is, he declares, "I am, I exist," and that fact remains true "each time that I pronounce it, or that I mentally conceive it."

"But what then am I?" Descartes asks himself, before rattling off a laundry list of possibilities. Finally, he deduces that he is "a real thing . . . a thing which thinks . . . a thing which doubts, understands, conceives, affirms, denies, wills, refuses, which also imagines and feels."

By Descartes's logic, any thinking thing must have the ability to entertain ideas, some innate, including the idea of God. Such ideas "cannot be assumed to be pure nothingness," as Descartes argues in the *Meditations,* and cannot be fabricated by the human mind. They are by nature true and immutable and caused by the thing itself. Thus the idea of God must arise from God, and God, therefore, must exist.

In all, Descartes spells out three proofs of God in the *Meditations* before turning his attention to the relationship of the human body to the human soul. By this point in the *Meditations,* Descartes has all but banished his self-imposed doubt and has begun his reconstruction of reality. He has proved that he exists, that God exists, and that the physical world exists. Now, in the sixth meditation, he sets out to prove that not only does he himself exist as a "thinking thing," but that the part of himself that thinks—his soul or mind—exists separately from the unthinking thing that harbors it, the body.

The mind, as Descartes has already shown, can be perceived through reason as a thinking thing, immaterial and unextended—in other words, invisible and not occupying space. By contrast, the body, as he now states, can only be perceived through the senses and is in every respect the soul's opposite—unthinking, material, and extended. Both body and soul, however, are so intermingled that they compose one whole, the true person. Moreover, the one can affect the other, so that an injury to the body results in pain registered by the mind, just as a conscious decision on the part of the mind can produce movement in the body. But such interaction does not mean dependence. "It is certain," writes Descartes, "that this I (that is to say, my soul by which I am what I am), is entirely and absolutely distinct from my body, and can exist without it." Granted; however, the question of exactly how a bodyless mind can affect a mindless body remains unanswered.

ear the end of his life, Descartes finally tackled the question in his *Treatise on the Passions of the Soul.* In this work, he ventures to locate the seat of the soul in the brain's pineal gland. In Descartes's opinion, this gland is the material link between the body he can see and the soul he cannot see—the arena where the two can, after all, interact. Through the pineal gland, the soul can "thrust" the animal spirits throughout the body and so move the muscles and nerves; likewise, the motions of the body can influence the mind through the same point of contact.

Philosophy disputed and science would later disprove most of the Cartesian notions about physiology, and science and philosophy were not Descartes's only critics. Religion had a dim view of him as well, taking up the cudgels to pummel Cartesian rationalism as a threat to the authority of the Church. Yet few detractors, secular or religious, were so elegant in their choice of insults as the theologian Blaise Pascal. "I cannot forgive Descartes," he sniffed contemptuously in response to Descartes's vision of a clockwork universe set in motion by an otherwise indifferent God. "He would have liked, in the whole of his philosophy, to be able to bypass God. But he could not help making Him give a shove to set the world in motion, after that he had nothing further to do with God."

The fact was that throughout his writings Descartes

had been condescending, and not exactly reassuring, toward the hierarchy of his own Catholic faith. Even so, it would seem that his various proofs of the existence of God might have earned him a permanent place in the Church's good graces. Such was not the case. Among other unorthodoxies, his advocacy of human free will and his insistence that reality could be deciphered through science rather than through divine revelation earned Descartes's works a place on the Church's Index of forbidden books in 1663. By then, however, the man who in life could give his heart only to truth was safely dead and his influence unstoppable.

Descartes's rationalism ushered in the Age of Enlightenment, the intellectual renaissance that set Europe and North America aglow in the seventeenth and eighteenth centuries. The Enlightenment challenged the theology-based social order by establishing reason as the most important source and test of truth. It was not long, however, before a new school of thought, empiricism, arose to downplay the importance of reason as the final arbiter of truth, especially in science. Truth, empiricism argued, should be sought only in sensory experience and tested against sensory experience. Only if a supposed fact could be verified by perception could it actually be true.

The empiricists—most notably the British empiricists John Locke, George Berkeley, and David Hume—functioned, each in his turn, as an engine of destruction bent on razing Cartesian rationalism, just as Descartes himself had pulled down his own generation's towers of accepted knowledge. In fact, as the first of the British empiricists, John Locke fancied himself "an under-laborer in clearing the ground a little, and removing some of the rubbish that lies in the way of knowledge." Locke acknowledges the "master builders whose mighty designs in advancing the sciences will leave lasting monuments to the admiration of posterity." But he is convinced the builders' time is past and that they must give way to the philosophical wrecking crew.

Still, this self-styled "under-laborer" had as much in common with the rationalists who preceded him as he did with the empiricists who followed. Like Descartes, for example, Locke thought matter as certain as the immaterial spirit and in his own *Essay concerning Human Understanding* describes a person as "a thinking intelligent being." In another passage that echoes Descartes, Locke characterizes bodies as "solid extended substances" perceived by the senses and the soul as "a substance that thinks" and is perceived by reflection.

However, unlike Descartes, Locke thought the interaction of mind and body "obscure and inconceivable." Moreover, if ideas were innate to Descartes, to Locke they were merely the product of sensory experience. In fact, Locke thought of the mind as a blank tablet on which experience, and experience alone, scribbled the thoughts, perceptions, and understandings that compose ideas.

he Irish-Anglican bishop George Berkeley took up the torch of empiricism from Locke in the early 1700s, but not without dousing the latter's belief in the existence of matter and igniting the fires of immaterialism. To empiricism's new torchbearer, the material world is not material at all but exists only in human perceptions: The tree exists only in the sense that you see it. Only minds and the perceptions of minds truly exist, and to be—to exist—is either to perceive or to be perceived. In this realm of the immaterial, Berkeley envisions the soul as an incorporeal, active substance that is always thinking, constantly absorbing and generating the ideas and perceptions that constitute both reality and imagination. Moreover, he says, the soul's activity does not cease with the body's death: The soul is immortal. God, Berkeley posits, is the factor whose power can make human perceptions orderly.

Despite the promise of immortality, Berkeley's readers were not wholly persuaded by his concept of immaterialism and were as likely as not to shrug off his conclusions as the wild imaginings of yet another comical Irishman. If so, those readers could only have been more amused when in

1744 Berkeley published *Siris,* a curious book that managed to combine a treatise on the supposed medicinal benefits of tar-water with the philosopher's own vision of an "ascent" from this world to that of the supernatural. By that time, however, the next chapter of empiricism was already being written. Its author was a Scotsman who as a boy was once described by his own mother as a "well-meanin' critter, but uncommon weak-minded."

It is beyond question that David Hume's mother proved to be a poor judge. The son she thought so intellectually ill-equipped went on to distinguish himself, in the words of the writer James Boswell, as "the greatest writer in Britain." Nevertheless, Hume's calling was for a time in doubt as he wavered between his family's desire that he become a lawyer and his own fondness for "books of reasoning and philosophy, and [for] poetry and the polite authors." The doubt ended when Hume experienced an epiphany, not unlike that of Descartes, which "opened up to me a new Scene of Thought." Hume's revelation grew out of his discovery of the philosophy of Francis Hutcheson, a fellow Scotsman whose works took issue with the then common belief that morality had its source in the Bible or in reason. Hutcheson contended that morality merely reflected society's perception of right and wrong and a particular individual's desire for approval or disapproval. If that were so, Hume speculated, might not all knowledge be rooted in our feelings of what is true? And if that be the case, is not everything that every human brain has ever learned merely an illusion? Hume suspected so and set out to prove it. But like Descartes's "marvelous science," Hume's "new Scene of Thought" would incubate for a decade, until finally in 1739 he published his *Treatise of Human Nature,* a work he would later revise as *An Enquiry concerning Human Understanding.*

To his dismay, the book that he had hoped would attract the attention of the world "fell dead-born from the press" amid a flurry of unfavorable reviews. But readers who ignored the reviews and took a chance on Hume discovered in his book a bold new philosophy that rejected the metaphysics of Plato, Thomas Aquinas, and Descartes as

"rash arrogance" and dismissed Cartesian substance as a "chimera." Moreover, Hume did for the mind what Berkeley had done for matter, denying the existence of a soul as thoroughly as his empiricist predecessor had denied the reality of the body. In its place, Hume argued what has come to be called the "bundle" concept—the belief that minds are "nothing but a bundle or collection of different perceptions, which succeed each other with an inconceivable rapidity, and are in a perpetual flux and movement."

Nowhere in this Humean vision of mind and matter is there room for reason as a source of truth that motivates moral conduct. Instead, upending Plato's metaphor of the charioteer and his recalcitrant horses, Hume contends that "reason is, and ought only to be, the slave of the passions, and can never pretend to any other office than to serve and obey them." In true empiricist fashion, Hume suggests that the only hope of penetrating reality lies in sense perception.

aving established perception as the only source of truth, Hume now sets out to prove it as the only test of it as well. He does this by dividing perceptions into impressions and ideas. Impressions, Hume writes, are our immediate sensations, passions, and emotions, what "we hear, or see, or feel, or love, or hate, or desire, or will." Ideas, on the other hand, are of less consequence, since they are only copies of impressions. It follows then that every idea arises out of an impression, and without an impression there can be no idea.

Hume's most enduring contribution to Western thought was to upend the Enlightenment's icon of science based on necessary causality. Empiricism rests on the idea that sensory perception is the only valid test of truth, and necessity cannot be perceived. Merely observing that things happen in a sequence does not prove that one thing necessarily causes another or that the sequence is necessarily a foregone conclusion. In other words, just because the sun rose today does not mean that it will rise tomorrow. We assume that it will, but we do not know it. Our assumption results from mere habit, a natural belief that something will necessarily happen based on the perception that it happened before. "Every effect is a distinct event from its cause," Hume warns, and, as such, any link between a cause and its supposed effect can have no basis in observation or experience. At best, causes and their effects are nothing more than a sequence of events linked by probability, not certainty. With this argument, Hume robs the universe of its necessary causal order and leaves perception as the basis of all knowledge.

Hume approaches the subject of immortality with the same skepticism, believing the human soul draws its breath through the body and the death of the body means the death of the soul. Even such a small death as sleep is a "temporary extinction" of the soul and just a preview of the eternal extinction to come once a particular body nods off for the last time. To Hume, "bare possibility" is a dim star to hitch one's hope of immortality to, and the very idea that "Agamemnon, Thersites, Hannibal, Varro and every stupid clown that ever existed in Italy, Scythia, Bactria or Guinea are now alive" seems utterly preposterous.

Even the approach of his own death failed to shake Hume's confidence in his belief that once dead, always dead. Indeed, as he lay on his deathbed during the summer of 1776, Hume was visited by James Boswell, the celebrated biographer of the more celebrated lexicographer Samuel Johnson. Boswell, a religious man despite an unbridled fondness for women and alcohol, was himself terrified of death and fearful of the eternal damnation his sins might have earned him. That any man, Hume included, could both deny the existence of God and reject the immortality of the soul was simply unthinkable to the excitable Boswell.

Convinced that the nearness of death would cure Hume of his skepticism, Boswell made it a point during his last interview with the dying philosopher to inquire if Hume had any second thoughts. "Don't you believe that there is life after death," the biographer began, "that your soul will live on after you are dead?"

Hume, the empiricist to the end, cheerfully admitted it was possible, just as it was possible that a lump of coal tossed into the nearby fire would not burn. "Possible," said Hume, "but there is no basis for believing it—not by reason, and not by sense perception, not by our experience." As Hume saw it, immortality seemed a most unreasonable fancy, if for no other reason than that it would have to apply equally to the intellectual and to the porter drunk on gin by midmorning. Even from a standpoint of practicality, immortality seemed unworkable. "The trash of every age must then be preserved," Hume stated, "and new universes must be created to contain such infinite numbers." Boswell, ever the believer, could only manage a lame response: "Mr. Hume, you know spirit does not take up space."

ix weeks after bidding Boswell a genial farewell, Hume went to his grave and, presumably, learned at last whether death was a sealed coffin or—as he thought most unlikely—an open door into a populous eternity. Like Descartes before him, Hume left behind a chorus of critics when he fled the world, many of whom would have nodded in agreement decades later when Ralph Waldo Emerson, who himself saw terror "attached to the name of Hume," accused Mrs. Hume's "well-meanin' critter" of committing an outrage against human nature. But neither death nor the disapproval of Hume's detractors could stem the tide of empiricism, and by the time the eighteenth century was drawing its own last breaths, the name of Hume, terror and all, was a name to be reckoned with.

Among those doing the reckoning was Immanuel Kant, a prestigious professor of philosophy at the University of Königsberg in East Prussia. Kant gave Hume credit for rousing him from his "dogmatic slumber." Yet he dedicated most of his waking years to an effort to lead philosophy away from Hume's skepticism and "into the safe road of a science." In fact, by 1781, just five years after Hume's death, Kant published his intellectually daunting *Critique of Pure*

Reason, the first of three major works that would synthesize Hume's empiricism and Descartes's rationalism into what Kant referred to as "critical philosophy." In these works, Kant affirms that knowledge is rooted in sense perception, as the empiricists said, but claims that the mind is no passive receptor; it imposes its own concepts on the sensations it receives. Ultimate reality (the thing-in-itself, or *Ding-in-sich*) is transcendent or beyond knowing.

Thus if Locke saw the mind as a blank sheet of paper, and Hume saw it as a stage across which impressions skittered and danced, Kant reserved a role for reason in his scheme of things. Reason, he maintains, is the source of a number of so-called pure concepts, or categories, which are preprogrammed into the mind itself. These categories form a kind of framework for knowledge by which the mind can organize impressions and give them meaning.

Kant's pure concepts made the laws of science again dependent on the mind, in effect restoring the rational order Hume had sought to destroy. Having done that, Kant set about restoring God and the soul's immortality. He did so by splitting the self in two: the observable self that science can know and the "noumenal" self that is a moral person. The moral self, says Kant, requires immortality if the soul is to continue struggling toward virtue. This self also requires that God exist to reward the virtuous with happiness they may not have had in life. Does this dual-self construct constitute proof that God exists and the soul lives on? Kant does not make this assertion; he shows only that the moral self is compelled to *assume* these comforting conclusions.

Kant's successor on the stage of German idealism, Georg Wilhelm Friedrich Hegel, had no such qualms regarding the nature of the soul and its survival in an afterlife. To Hegel, the body is property designed to be occupied and used by the soul, itself a free entity and the "essence" of a person. Moreover, the soul is inseparable from the body, at least in this life. "While I am alive," Hegel wrote in his monumental *Philosophy of Right,* published in 1821, "my soul (the concept and, to use a higher term, the free entity) and my body are not separated." Once death has dissolved the

A Multitude of Minds

After René Descartes divided all things into soul and body, or mind and matter, one of his successors in the seventeenth-century European arena of ideas simplified the equation with a singular notion: There is no matter. For German philosopher and mathematician Gottfried Wilhelm Leibniz, there was only mind. What seems to be inert matter, according to Leibniz, is only a stupid variety of mind.

Leibniz speculated that all apparent matter is made up of basic bits of mind called monads. Monad types are nearly endless in number, he said, and are strewn along a scale of lesser to greater intelligence. A rock is made up of very dumb monads, while a microbe has smarter monads, and a mammal has brighter ones still. Higher on the scale are humans, then angels. Finally there is God, with the highest sort of monads—a special case in that He is infinite and the creator of all other monads, which are finite.

Leibniz saw no difference in kind among finite monads—only in degree. Thus a rock and a person are the same thing—mind—and greater intelligence is all that distinguishes the latter from the former.

The Way of All Souls

"Easy is the descent to hell," wrote the Roman poet Virgil in the first century BC. The ascent to heaven, on the other hand, has most often been described as tortuous. Since ancient times, many cultures have viewed the whole of human existence as one long journey, with heaven, or spiritual perfection, as the soul's ultimate destination.

For some, the voyage begins when the body dies. The Guarayo Indians of Bolivia, for instance, once believed that after death the soul faced two paths, one easily navigated, the other more demanding. Only by choosing and surviving the perilous route would the soul achieve eternal happiness.

For other faiths, including Christianity, it is one's earthly life, with all its associated trials and tribulations, that represents the soul's tumultuous journey toward enlightenment. John Bunyan's seventeenth-century allegory *Pilgrim's Progress* follows an everyman by the name of Christian as he navigates a symbolic landscape that is littered with diversions designed to lure him from the path to salvation. As depicted in the nineteenth-century engraving shown below, the wayfarer's route from the earthly City of Destruction to the Celestial City, or heaven, is replete with such temptations and obstacles as Vanity Fair, the Valley of Humiliation, and the River of Death.

The spiral shape of the path, perhaps representing the windings of human life, is a symbol common to mystic interpretations of the soul's quest. In cabalistic thought, for instance, the soul spirals down the tree of life and assumes a physical presence at the time of birth. At death, the process is reversed, and the soul returns to the spiritual realm. For some New Age thinkers, the spiral is symbolic of the cycles of nature—the changing seasons, the waxing and waning moon, the ebbing and flowing tides—as well as a gently curving path toward complete knowledge.

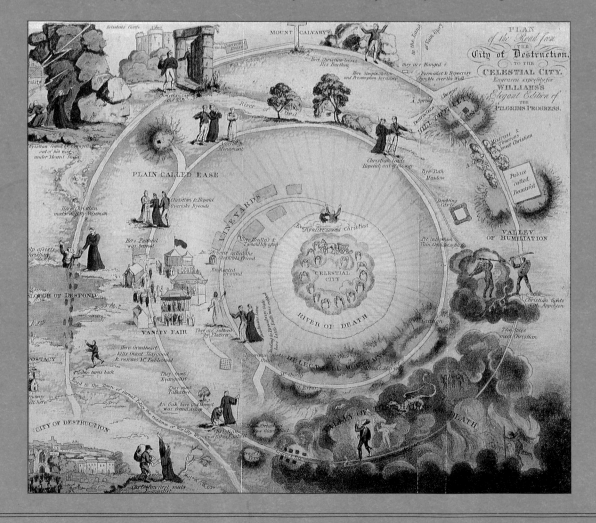

link between body and soul, however, the soul is freed to be swallowed up in the Absolute, Hegel's concept of an all-encompassing Universal Spirit that knows no past and no future but lives in "an essential now."

Whether the individual human soul is enveloped in this Absolute at death and loses its individuality in the process or lives on as part of the Absolute remains a matter of some conjecture; Hegel is unclear on this point. What is certain is that Hegel conceives of the Absolute as the indwelling soul of the cosmos and not as the architect and Unmoved Mover of a clockwork universe, as Descartes and Aristotle had maintained. Incorporated and unified in this Absolute is the totality of all the rational truths of logic, science, psychology, history, politics, art, religion, and philosophy. The result is a "self-comprehending totality," an ultimate reality within which "the real is the rational" and "the truth is the Whole." The Absolute, Hegel says, is "being, eternal life, self-knowing truth, and it is all truth." The Absolute is a God who is the soul of the world and exists within it. His is the only soul that transcends death.

Hegel, whose life bridged the eighteenth and nineteenth centuries, viewed his epoch as "a birth-time and a period of transition" when the spirit of man was parting from the old order of things and old ways of thinking. In the mid-nineteenth century, nowhere was that assessment more applicable than North America. There, in transplanted form, idealism had sprouted as New England transcendentalism and was challenging the conventions of colonial thought. From transcendentalism, in turn, would spring a host of reform movements, social causes, and literary works amounting to a repudiation of the established order.

At the head of this intellectual movement stood the imposing figure of Ralph Waldo Emerson, whose slim volume *Nature* appeared in 1836 and quickly became a kind of transcendentalist manifesto. In its pages, Emerson pictures the universe divided into two realms, the first an unreal world of appearances and sensations, and the second an unseen transcendental realm presided over by the mind and the soul. The former can be discovered by perception,

writes Emerson, but the latter, the world of ultimate reality, is best approached through poetry and philosophy.

Elsewhere in the essay Emerson describes the soul as "the apparition of God, . . . the organ through which the universal spirit speaks to the individual, and strives to lead back the individual to it." Through this soul, humanity can surmount the facade of ordinary experience and understanding and commune directly with God. Matter, in contrast, is "a phenomenon, not a substance," and the material world "a divine dream, from which we may presently awake to the glories and certainties of day."

uch thoughts echo others recorded earlier in Emerson's diary, among them an entry that detects "a correspondence between the human soul and everything that exists in the world" and another in which Emerson confides that "the highest revelation is that God is in every man." Despite such sentiments and despite Emerson's efforts to shape them into a philosophy, transcendentalism resisted formal definition. It remained as much a state of mind as a philosophy, a will-o'-the-wisp whose character was best described by one of its followers as "an enthusiasm, a wave of sentiment, a breath of mind that caught up such as were prepared to receive it, elated them, transported them, and passed on—no man knowing whither it went."

Whatever its attributes, transcendentalism attracted some of the foremost thinkers and writers of the time. Notable among them were that most diffident of different drummers, essayist Henry David Thoreau; feminist and literary critic Margaret Fuller; the mystic and educationist Bronson Alcott, and George Ripley, the founder of Brook Farm, one of several utopian communities that drew on transcendentalist ideas. They and many other like-minded individualists heeded Emerson's call to "enjoy an original relation to the universe" and confront God and nature face to face. For these disciples, Emerson's *Nature* was both gospel and creed, and most of them, if not all, could identify with Emerson as he put his own preaching into practice: "Standing on the bare ground, my head bathed by the blithe air, and uplifted into infinite space,—all mean egotism vanishes. I become a transparent eyeball; I am nothing; I see all; the currents of the Universal Being circulate through me; I am part or particle of God."

In later works, Emerson goes on to develop his concept of the individual human soul and of what he calls "that Unity, that Over-soul, within which every man's particular being is contained and made one with all others." In the essay "The Over-Soul," for example, the philosopher identifies the individual soul as "the background of our being," the master of the intellect, and the will and the power that animate the body. To this spirit, all the world and all of society are as transient as mist, for the soul, "the immortal pupil," as Emerson refers to it in *Nature,* has its eyes elsewhere. "The soul looketh steadily forwards," writes Emerson in "The Over-Soul," "creating a world before her, leaving worlds behind her."

The oversoul, like Hegel's Absolute, embraces all and everything and reveals itself to every human soul sensitive to the spiritual and poetic dimensions of life. It is the soul of the universe; unseen and deathless, permeating and enveloping each soul. From it every soul flows as water from a sea, and to it, at death, every soul returns. "Man," writes Emerson, "is a stream whose source is hidden."

The image of the soul as water also figures in the works of William James, the noted American psychologist and philosopher who struggled with an ongoing dilemma of modern science: the knotty question of whether an insubstantial entity—a mind, or soul, or consciousness—is distinguishable or separable from the physical brain. For all his grappling with the issue, James never seemed satisfied with his own conclusions. On the one hand, he was a leading exponent of the theory of neutral monism. According to this doctrine, all things are composed of the same neutral "stuff," and depending on the context, this primal stuff can be mental or material. It can be mind or brain.

Often, however, James seemed uneasy with this solution to the problem of mind-body dualism and inclined to side with the materialist view that mind is merely a function of brain. In his landmark 1890 text, *The Principles of Psychology,* James describes how the mind exudes thought as a "stream of consciousness," implying that consciousness is only a product of the physical brain. "The bald fact," he writes, "is that *when the brain acts, a thought occurs,"* and that process needs no spiritual input to be complete.

ere James was writing not only as a psychologist, but as an advocate of pragmatism, the philosophy that measures truth by its consequences for human life. Since the soul cannot be seen to have consequences, it is a "complete superfluity," in this Jamesian view. To those who would extend the notion of consciousness to encompass the attributes of soul—of consciousness as something transcending the brain—he is less than charitable. They are merely taking refuge, he says, in a "spiritual chloroform" that only temporarily silences doubt. Elsewhere in *The Principles of Psychology,* James discounts all arguments aimed at proving the need for a soul. "The passing thought itself is the only *verifiable* thinker, and its empirical connection with the brain-process is the ultimate known law." As for the prospects for immortality, he has little hope: "My final conclusion, then, about the substantial Soul is that it explains nothing and guarantees nothing."

But this conclusion also left James restless. The son of a believer in the Swedish mystic Emanuel Swedenborg, James had been bemused throughout his life by the abstractions of faith—God and the soul among them. However didactic his pronouncements on these matters, he seemed unable to stop wrestling with them. This became increasingly true when, in midlife, he became fascinated with Spiritualism and its claim that the souls of the dead can commune with the living. As a psychical investigator, James strayed far afield from the strictures that bound him as a psychologist or as a philosopher. And the freewheeling metaphysical theories he advanced won little note from his adherents in either field, even while they endeared him to parapsychologists.

His new speculations were apparent in a lecture on immortality that he delivered at Harvard University in 1898. James spoke of the threshold that separates the mind from the brain, likening it to a dam and comparing consciousness to a mother sea. Every now and then, he said, waves of thought spill over the dam, flooding the brain and allowing its owner to tap into the oneness of the universe. These floods, James mused, might account for such psychic phenomena as clairvoyance and ghostly apparitions, as well as for religious conversions and the "transference of thought" between the living and the dead.

Taking issue with his own earlier conclusions, James conceded that it was "not at all impossible, but on the contrary quite possible" that the soul's life may still continue once the brain is dead. Admittedly, as he himself had written in 1890, the brain's function is to think, and thought is its output, spewing like steam from a teakettle. But, James said now, thinking only accounts for the brain's productive function. It does not explain its so-called transmissive function, its capacity to experience reality as "glows of feeling, glimpses of insight, and streams of knowledge and perception." James asked his listeners to imagine that a veil separates the seen world of the actual from the unseen world of ultimate reality. They were to envision their brains as thin and opaque places in the veil. "What will happen?" he asked the crowd. Is it not possible, he answered himself, that the "white radiance of eternity," as the poet Shelley put it, may penetrate the veil from the other side, that a flood of spiritual energy will pour through each thin and half-transparent place represented by a human brain? And is it not just as possible that even when our brains are dead, "the sphere of being that supplied the consciousness would still be intact; and in that more real world . . . the consciousness might, in ways unknown to us, continue still?"

James gave his audience a moment to ponder an answer before going on himself to confront a second stumbling block in the path of immortality, one that had also troubled Hume a century earlier: the glut of humanity, preserved eternally, that must surely strain the capacity of any heaven. But James nimbly leaped the hurdle of an overpopulated afterlife by informing his listeners that each new mind brings with it "its own room to inhabit; and these spaces never crowd each other—the space of my imagination, for example, in no way interferes with yours." James was also quick to remind believers in the crowd that an infinite God is infinitely expandable and "has so inexhaustible a capacity for love that His call and need is for a literally endless accumulation of created lives."

hile not, of course, proving the soul's immortality, James's lecture at least held open its possibility. A few years later, he hinted even more strongly of his hope in a hereafter in noting the sudden death of a colleague: "Too bad, too bad!" he wrote. "And the manliest, unworldliest, kindliest of human beings. May he still be *energizing* somewhere." James wanted desperately to believe that the human soul survives the death of the body. Nevertheless, he confessed that he had found not a shred of evidence to sustain that hope, even after years of interest in psychic research. His despair sounds clearly in the final lines of an essay that was the last of his works published in his lifetime. "There is no conclusion," he writes. "There are no fortunes to be told, and there is no advice to be given.—Farewell!"

For at least one of James's contemporaries, the British philosopher John M'Taggart Ellis M'Taggart, any last farewell would have to have taken the form of a "see you later." M'Taggart, though an atheist, was nevertheless a firm believer in an afterlife—or afterlives. He saw this life as just one of many, each bounded fore and aft by birth and death. M'Taggart's "doctrine of a plurality of lives" declares that each person has at least three lives—the present one, an earlier one, and a future one. These last two are guaran-

teed by the philosopher's certainty of both preexistence and personal immortality. But in all probability, he suggests, each of us has many more lives than three—many before the present one and many beyond it.

For M'Taggart, who followed his own brand of Hegelian idealism, reality is entirely spiritual, consisting of individual minds and their contents. In this view, material objects only appear to be real. Actually, they too are minds and parts of the contents of minds. Time and space are also unreal in M'Taggart's scheme of things. Ultimate reality will only emerge when the appearance of time has at last ticked its final tock, and the apparent universe has dissolved into what M'Taggart envisions as a "timeless and endless state of love." In this realm of perpetual rapture, he believes, we shall "know nothing but our beloved, those they love, and ourselves loving them."

Such a picture of a timeless hereafter, though idyllic, would have been laughable to Bertrand Russell, M'Taggart's most famous Cambridge classmate. To Russell the only time is now and the only hereafter is here, and neither preexistence nor immortality has any foundation in fact. "All the evidence goes to show," Russell wrote in *Why I Am Not a Christian,* "that what we regard as our mental life is bound up with brain structure and organized body energy. Therefore it is rational to suppose that mental life ceases when bodily life ceases."

Both Russell's belief in God and his hope in immortality had died before he ever set foot on the Cambridge grounds in 1890. Once there, he fell briefly under the influence of the slightly older M'Taggart, "more or less" swallowing M'Taggart's concept of the Absolute as well as the other tenets of the British brand of Hegelian idealism. Russell even took "curious pleasure" in mentally dissolving time, space, and matter, and in imagining that the entire universe was nothing but mind.

But such pleasures proved ephemeral, and by 1898, Russell had abandoned idealism and adopted what he called a "watered-down" version of Platonism. That, too, proved unsatisfactory—"nonsense," in fact—to the nimble-minded Russell, who went on to adopt and discard empiricism before settling on his own philosophy, which he called logical atomism. Logical atomism holds that the basis of all knowledge is the data of sensory observation. Out of this base is built the logical structure of science.

Russell was, at one time, a mind-matter dualist. However, as he analyzed his views under the lamp of logical atomism, he came to believe that mind and matter are not separate substances but the same kind of neutral sense experiences, or sensa, structured differently. This view, the subject of his 1921 book, *The Analysis of Mind,* corresponds to the neutral monism of William James. In a departure from the Jamesian concept, Russell comes to view his sensa as a unique kind of physical process in the nervous system. Russell, who thought "mental life bound up with brain structure," had no problem identifying with materialism. "I still think," he wrote as late as 1959 when he was eighty-seven, "that man is cosmically unimportant, and that a Being, if there were one, who could view the universe impartially, without the bias of *here* and *now,* would hardly mention man, except perhaps in a footnote at the end of the volume."

Russell's views on immortality, bleak to some and realistic to others, were in any case long-lived. In a life that spanned nearly a century, Russell not only influenced the course of Western philosophy but, more immediately, the thinking of some of his more celebrated students at Cambridge. Among them were the Austrian-born mathematician and philosopher Ludwig Wittgenstein and the British moral philosopher C. D. Broad.

Wittgenstein, who was himself somewhat instrumental in shaping Russell's evolving philosophy of logical atomism, came to Cambridge in 1911 specifically to study mathematics under Russell. For his part, Russell was impressed by the intensity of his new student and by his "fire and penetration and intellectual purity." Wittgenstein's ability to absorb knowledge was no less impressive, and according to Russell, the young Austrian "soon knew all that I had to teach." Russell was probably not exaggerating, for Wittgenstein went on to become one of the most influential philosophers of modern times, one whose thought would dominate the field in the twentieth century. This fact is not without irony, since Wittgenstein proposed that there is little in the world more useless than philosophy itself.

Wittgenstein contends that philosophers should not be discussing the soul at all—or, for that matter, any of the other ideas that constitute the content of philosophy—because in doing so they are only creating problems that do not exist. Philosophy is futile, he says, because it is awash in linguistic confusion. Wittgenstein contends that language must be particular to a context, to the "form of life" in which it is used. Thus there is an everyday language that most people speak, a language for dentists, one for farmers, one for surgeons, and so forth. Wittgenstein likens these languages to games, each with its own rules that must be followed if statements are to have any meaning. Philosophy's dilemma is that it has no language of its own and that it abuses other languages. In trying to reach truths about the nature of reality, Wittgenstein says, philosophers violate the rules of ordinary language by stretching and bending it in extraordinary ways. They also mix languages—borrowing from the tongues of sociology, psychology, and physics, for instance—and creating in the process a jumbled and useless potpourri. The result is that they create nonproblems, grapple with nonissues, postulate nonfacts. In short, they babble. They can say nothing of the soul or God or the human condition that can have any meaning. God and the soul are nonproblems.

His mission, Ludwig Wittgenstein believed, was to show the fly the way out of the philosophical fly bottle—to rescue, in fact, philosophers from philosophy. Still, he realized the virtual impossibility—not to mention the irony—of the task. He saw his own "absurd job" as a professor of philosophy as "a kind of living death." Philosophy, he said, is in need of linguistic therapy for its anxieties about God

English philosopher C. D. Broad—who twice served as the president of the Society for Psychical Research—thought that studies of paranormal phenomena might prove his theory that mental events can survive the death of the body.

and the soul. And what the therapy should aim for is a kind of suicide. Philosophy's only valid goal, according to Wittgenstein, is to do away with itself.

Individual death, for Wittgenstein, was yet another nonproblem. Even as a young man he could state that "death is not an event in life" because, from a strictly logical point of view, death is not lived through. So much for the soul's survival.

C. D. Broad's outlook on the afterlife was equally dour. Personally, he had no desire to survive his own death and would have been content to know that death was a binding contract devoid of any spiritual loopholes through which the soul could wriggle into the hereafter. But unlike his mentor Bertrand Russell, Broad held that immortality might at least be logically possible and might even be proved empirically, perhaps through psychic research. His own solution to the mind-body problem is "a variant of the Platonic-Cartesian view," as he describes it, a variant that sees every human being as an "intimate compound of two constituents, one being his ordinary everyday body, and the other being something of a very different kind, not open to ordinary observation, . . . a Ψ-component."

This Ψ-, or psi, component, or "psychogenic factor," can be modified by a person's life experiences, Broad believes, and can survive the body's death. Moreover, the Ψ-component need not be unextended and incorporeal, like Descartes's thinking thing, but can be a physical, if invisible, presence. Comparing the Ψ-component to the unheard sounds or actual sound waves of a radio broadcast, Broad suggests that a person can exist after death, just as those

The Karmic Key

In religions that predominate in the East, the concept of the human soul is inextricable from a belief in reincarnation. Rebirth is a central tenet of both Hinduism and Buddhism. In the Buddhist view, the soul is chained to an ever-turning wheel of birth, death, and rebirth. Each rebirth is dictated by karma—the fate decreed for the next life by one's behavior in the current one. Karma dictates punishment or reward. Malevolent acts and materialistic pursuits are thought to create negative karma that might entail a soul's return in a wretched human state or even in some form less than human. Virtue and discipline, both mental and physical, enhance karma, boding well for the soul's progress toward loosing itself from the inexorable wheel. Escaping the wheel is the ultimate goal of all souls, for to end the cycle of reincarnation is to achieve enlightenment, the shedding of all illusions. With enlightenment comes blissful union with the cosmic oneness.

Karma is sometimes described in material terms as the residue of one's actions, an elusive substance that combines with unfulfilled desires after death and guides the soul in its journey from one body to the next. This aspect of karma greatly influences the thinking of the Jains, a small but important sect in India.

Jainism traditionally describes the soul, or jiva, as a pure, colorless, and transparent energy. All things in the universe —humans, animals, plants, even rocks—are believed to possess jiva, which is by nature blissful and intelligent. However, the karmic residue stirred up in the material world is thought to cling like dust to the jiva, staining and clouding it with colors that correspond to the anger, hate, or love that motivates one's thoughts and deeds. Gentleness and selflessness attract light, clear colors to the jiva; malice and selfishness—and above all, violence—taint it with shades that are dark and muddy.

Jains believe that the conditions of rebirth depend on the amount and color of karma adhering to the jiva. Heavy, brooding karma may consign its bearer to rebirth as an animal or a demon. But virtuous thoughts and acts, combined with the repudiation of worldly goals, help cleanse the jiva, eventually leading it to enlightenment.

Since a deep respect for all life, even the lowest forms, is a key belief of their religion, Jains go to great lengths to avoid harming any living being. They are strict vegetarians, of course, but their concern for life extends well beyond not eating meat. For example, they do not drink water after dark lest they accidentally swallow an insect. Pesky flies and mosquitos are not harmed; indeed, letting them bite is considered a positive karmic act.

Jain monks carry nonviolence even further. They wear cloths over their mouths to avoid disturbing the atoms of the air and carry a broom to sweep the ground before them so as not to inadvertently crush small insects: Even unintentional destruction can dim the jiva. If a monk should fall into a river, he must not swim with slicing strokes to the shore but only float gently in order not to injure the atoms of the water.

The cut-out figure in this eighteenth-century brass Jain icon symbolizes a believer's ultimate goal—the release of the jiva, or soul, from the cycle of birth, death, and rebirth.

sounds or sound waves exist somewhere in space, even if the transmitter is destroyed.

It is also Broad's contention that such paranormal phenomena as out-of-the-body experiences and mediumistic communication support his psychogenic theory, providing the best evidence that humans are both mind and matter. Evidence of reincarnation, if it can be proved, will also shore up his dualistic theory, Broad contends. In fact, he considers reincarnation "the most plausible form of the doctrine of survival," albeit not the only form.

Regarding the quality of an afterlife, Broad assumes the existence of a Ψ-component and postulates several alternative possibilities for its fate. The most likely one, he claims, is a disembodied state that lasts until the Ψ-component is again united to a living body. But while personally banking on the possibility of a disembodied and dreamless afterlife, Broad hedges his bet by noting that the numerous reports of paranormal phenomena offer evidence of survival with at least some memory of a prior existence and provide a glimpse of heaven as a sea of Ψ-components and "non-human flotsam and jetsam."

In adopting his own brand of dualism, Broad stipulates that some compound of mind and matter, some kind of "ghost-in-the-machine," is absolutely essential to explain the survival of a human personality after death. That criterion, while conjuring up visions of some sort of spiritual-jack-in-a-material-box, was Broad's response to Gilbert Ryle, the British philosopher who a decade earlier had scorned Cartesian dualism as "the dogma of the Ghost in the Machine."

Ryle's attack took the form of a book, *The Concept of Mind,* in which the author disputes what he calls "the official doctrine" of dualism, Descartes's belief that every person exists on a physical and a mental plane and somehow survives death as a mental substance. Despite the length and the vehemence of his written attack, Ryle is willing to concede that the mind might exist. But if it does, it is as the form of the body, as its organizing principle. It does not exist as some unseen substance in a parallel universe ungoverned by the mechanical laws that apply to the body in this world. Instead, "to talk of a person's mind," says Ryle, "is to talk of the person's abilities, liabilities and inclinations to do and undergo certain sorts of things, and of the doing and undergoing of these things in the ordinary world."

The widely accepted belief that a place called the mind can exist apart from the body is as ludicrous to Ryle as believing that a separate, invisible place called the university can exist apart from the various buildings, playing fields,

Celestial Couriers

"Good night, sweet prince, and flights of angels sing thee to thy rest!" Thus Horatio bade the slain Hamlet farewell with the old but persistent image of angels bearing the dead to heaven. Since well before the time of Shakespeare, religion and folklore have associated angels with the care and the guidance of human beings on earth—as well as human souls in the afterlife.

Both the Old and New Testaments in the Bible abound with references to angels, who primarily act as divine messengers through whom God communicates with humankind; indeed, the word *angel* is the English translation of the Greek word meaning messenger. The wings adorning the myriad images of angels throughout the ages symbolize their role as celestial couriers.

Early Judeo-Christian theology expanded the roles of angels, particularly as caretakers of the soul. The Angel of Repentance reminded humans of their sins and promised forgiveness. After the death of the body, the Angel of Peace carried worthy souls to paradise. Each individual was believed to be watched over in life by a guardian angel—to whom, some thought, the soul would owe an accounting after death.

Angels figure prominently in Islamic tradition as well. In a variation of the guardian-angel theme, the Koran assigns every individual two angels: one to record good deeds and the other to note evil ones. Souls of the dead are thought to encounter a second pair of angels known as the examiners. Armed with whips of iron and fire, these fierce beings interrogate souls about their lives on earth in order to determine whether they merit entry to heaven.

Speculation about the nature of angels thrived in the Middle Ages and continues to this day. Some people believe that angels are the souls of those who die and go to heaven. However, most theologians and philosophers —in the past and even to-day—consider these beings to be pure, nonhuman spirits, created by God to manifest divine will. One contemporary thinker, the American philosopher Mortimer Adler, postulates that angels are minds without bodies, which assume human guise only as a function of their earthly ministry. When their tasks are finished, he suggests, they return to heaven, shedding along the way every last vestige of corporeality.

and other physical entities that compose it. It simply is not possible, Ryle argues, and there is no "ghost mysteriously ensconced in a machine." Nor, for that matter, can a man be considered a machine. "He might, after all, be a sort of animal," Ryle concludes, "namely, a higher mammal."

If at times it seemed that British philosophers were content to bicker over whether a human mind is or is not a ghost in a machine, across the English Channel in France writer and philosopher Jean-Paul Sartre was grappling with another Cartesian icon: the cogito itself. For nearly three centuries the cogito had stood as the Excalibur of philosophy, defying every attempt to dislodge it from the rock of truth. "I think, therefore I am." Who could deny it?

Sartre could, and with the support of the existentialist movement, he did. Gripping the cogito by its figurative hilt, he slipped it free of what, it now seemed, had only been the illusion of truth. Suddenly, the cogito could be seen for what it really was—a fallacy, at least from Sartre's point of view. Existence does not depend on the essence of a "thinking thing," and a person does not exist simply because he thinks. To the contrary, opines Sartre, existence precedes essence, and existence itself is the indubitable fact: I am, therefore I think.

Sartre and existentialism declare that far from affirming the certain existence of a thinking substance, all the cogito did was prove the certainty of consciousness—consciousness in the mere sense of awareness, not as an animating or immortal soul. A person exists not as some Platonic essence or as a Cartesian "thinking thing" or even as part and particle of some transcendental oversoul. A person exists as pure consciousness. Moreover, that consciousness is not directed at itself, as a substance that thinks, but outward toward reality. Consciousness itself is nothing; it exists only insofar as it is conscious of objects and of itself as being conscious of them.

Being and nothingness became, for Sartre, the touchstones of existence and the title of what is arguably his most important book. Within the pages of *Being and Noth-*

A protective angel cradles an infant representing the human soul in this detail from "Poème de l'Âme"—a cycle of poems and paintings concerning the soul by Louis Janmot, a French artist of the 1800s.

Fate or Free Will?

Confronted by a fork in the road, the man below deliberates over which path to follow. Both avenues appear open; where his life leads is up to him—or is it? Will his choice be truly his, or is it in fact a foregone conclusion? The question is age-old but still widely argued: Does fate or free will govern human existence?

Belief in free will is the conviction that humans are able to choose their course of action and that they are ultimately responsible for their choices. The philosophy of existentialism extends the concept to its limits, maintaining that free will is the basic reality—indeed the defining characteristic—of human existence. People live in a world shaped by their own choices, creating a reality that they are continually free to change.

On the other hand, determinism—the doctrine of fate—holds that everything that happens, including so-called acts of human will, results automatically from preexistent forces. And since all decisions are caused by natural or social laws beyond individual control, the freedom to choose is illusory, and thus, so is moral accountability.

Many philosophies have developed compromises between the two extremes. One middle ground was proposed by Baruch Spinoza, a Dutch philosopher of the seventeenth century. Spinoza thought that human actions are shaped by the past but that the exercise of imagination and reason can turn past experience into foresight, thereby enabling one to create one's own future.

In the twentieth century, some thinkers have compared the concept of human free will with that of biological choice. They postulate that choice belongs to all living things, whose ultimate aim is to survive. For example, although bacteria placed in the enzyme lactose always make one particular protein, they do have alternatives. If invaded by a virus, say, they can manufacture some other protein. The decision here is determined by environmental factors outside the control of the bacteria, but given those factors, choice is nevertheless still possible. So it is with human beings, whose range of choice, though not unlimited, is vastly greater than that of lowly bacteria.

In theology, the choice-fate controversy takes the form of free will versus predestination: whether the soul's final outcome depends on one's personal efforts to achieve salvation or is instead decided in advance by divine will. Saint Augustine addressed the issue as early as the fifth century, and the debate goes on to this day.

ingness, Sartre lays down the tenets of his philosophy, one that takes as its centerpiece the idea of human freedom. "Man secretes his own nothingness," Sartre writes, and it is that nothingness that betokens freedom, the freedom every person has to determine his or her own course and to give meaning to the world. According to Sartre, each of us is ultimately responsible for every aspect of our existence. There is no God to rely on, no Hegelian Absolute to mingle with. We are, in Sartre's words, "condemned to be free," and condemned, too, to suffer the anguish of this freedom, its loneliness, helplessness, and alienation. Freedom is to be untethered to any meaning that is imposed by the world or by any higher order, and even to be without external guideposts for one's own thoughts and decision

The only escape from this terrible freedom is down the dishonorable avenue of what Sartre calls "bad faith," the self-deception of pretending we are not free and not responsible for what we are and do. But this, says Sartre, is "a lie in the soul."

In the end, as Sartre wrote in the novel *Nausea,* life itself is nothing less than absurdity and death nothing more than the final nothingness, the ultimate obliteration of consciousness: "Every existing thing is born without reason, prolongs itself out of weakness and dies by chance."

Sartre's gloomy conclusion was not, of course, philosophy's last word on the matter of the soul. The debate goes on and is sure to continue indefinitely—a point that arose during the Great Soul Trial in Arizona. Philosophy did not go unrepresented in that peculiar proceeding, for the Arizona Board of Regents, desirous of setting up a chair of phi-

losophy at one of the state universities for the express purpose of pondering the soul, laid claim to James Kidd's money. But attorneys representing other interests pointed out that for all their centuries of plumbing the depths of the riddle, philosophers had failed to produce so much as an incontrovertible definition for the soul, much less a definitive road map of its fate. At best, they had provided only frameworks for considering it, ways of thinking about it, and endless arguments regarding its existence, its essence, and its outcome.

Summing up this point, one lawyer declared that "philosophers know nothing about the soul, have come up with nothing about the soul, and have no reasonable chance in the next 2,300 years of finding anything more than confused concepts of the soul if they receive the money." Philosopher Wittgenstein would probably have agreed, and so, apparently, did the trial judge. In the courtroom quest for the soul, the philosophers were never really in the running.

From Hell to Heaven

When the *Divine Comedy* was published early in the fourteenth century, the epic poem recounted a journey in the afterlife so vividly that many readers believed the writer, Dante Alighieri, had actually made the trip and returned to tell about it. Nor did the power of the Florentine poet's verse fade with the passage of time. Its images of possible fates awaiting the soul became stereotypes that persist to this day.

If Dante left little to the imagination about the horrors of the inferno, the uncertainties of purgatory, and the glories of paradise, artist Gustave Doré left nothing at all. Between 1861 and 1868, the great French illustrator, like many artists before him, undertook to give form to Dante's words. The results include the engravings reproduced on the following fifteen pages. The eerie majesty of Doré's pictures made them easily the most famous and memorable of all the illustrations to accompany the *Divine Comedy*. At right, for instance, Doré depicts the souls of the dead cowering before the mountainous Minos, the hellish half man, half beast who will judge them on the basis of their own confession, in which truth is compelled, and consign them to their appropriate torments in hell.

Dante, who wrote the *Comedy* over a fifteen-year period in his middle age, begins his first-person tale on the evening of Good Friday in the year 1300. Finding himself lost in a dark forest, he is rescued by his literary hero, the Roman poet Virgil, who tells Dante that his lost love, Beatrice, awaits him in heaven. A real Beatrice did exist, a girl who was Dante's childhood love. She died young. Virgil's mission, he tells his fellow poet, is to guide Dante to her. The arduous journey will take the poets through the ravages of hell and the rigors of purgatory before Dante can encounter Beatrice and ascend with her to the sublime heights of paradise.

One of the most extraordinary aspects of Dante's vision is the concreteness he lends to the three afterworlds, each of which comprises a separate book of the *Comedy*. Each realm has a complete architecture. The inferno, for example, is not some amorphous sulphurous pit, but a precisely structured chasm that lies directly below Jerusalem and extends down to the center of the earth. The mountain of purgatory rises out of the southern hemisphere directly opposite Jerusalem, and above its summit is paradise.

Abandon Hope, All Ye Who Enter Here is the dread warning inscribed in stone above the mouth of hell. The inferno has two areas, nether hell and upper hell, and is further divided into nine circles. Each accommodates particular kinds of sinners and degrees of wickedness. The loathsomeness of the sin and the severity of commensurate punishment increase with the depth of the abyss.

In upper hell, Dante and Virgil meet first the good pagans in limbo, and then, as the poets descend, they encounter those guilty of lust, gluttony, avarice, and anger—all sins caused by a lack of self-control, rather than ill will. More abominable still are the inhabitants of nether hell, beginning with the heretics who are entombed in fiery graves within the city of Dis. Further down are those who sinned through violence. In the fire and ice of nether hell's lowest circles shriek souls corrupted by fraud or malice. Among them are murderers and thieves, hypocrites, flatterers, sorcerers, corrupt politicians, seducers, panderers, and—worst of all—betrayers of trust. At the pit's core, Satan, supreme traitor against heaven, gnaws on the head of Judas Iscariot, supreme traitor among mortals—the betrayer of Christ.

Leaving the realm of utter despair, the poets cross a river and start up the mount of purgatory, where hope still exists. Purgatory has four parts—antepurgatory, lower purgatory, middle purgatory, and upper purgatory—and seven ledges. As in the inferno, the subdivisions of purgatory are meant for various degrees and types of sin—infractions that are in all cases less dire than those that sent sinners to hell. For example, the seven winding ledges, as they go upward, represent in decreasing severity the seven deadly sins: pride, envy, anger, sloth, greed, gluttony, and lust. Inhabitants of purgatory include sinners who repented at the moment of death, mortals who died unbaptized, and those whose material concerns on earth left them little time to contemplate God. All were less evil than weak. In purgatory they do not suffer torment; rather, they are encouraged by angels toward godly behavior and an understanding of their mistakes in life. If they attain a state of complete remorse and confess all of their faults, they are allowed to enter heaven. If they refuse or fail to correct the error of their ways, they are condemned to the inferno for all of eternity.

Having made his own sincere confession, Dante arrives at the summit of purgatory and crosses Lethe, the cleansing river of forgetfulness. On the other side he is reunited with Beatrice, who guides him into paradise. The celestial realm is divided into nine concentric heavens that rotate around the earth. Surrounding them all is the empyrean, an outermost heaven composed of light, reason, and love. In paradise, souls ascend in goodness toward the empyrean, where, disembodied, they live as auras of pure love and wisdom. The blessed enjoy, according to their merits, the vision of God. In the empyrean, Beatrice leaves Dante and ascends to her seat of glory, while Saint Bernard appears and explains to the poet the central mysteries of Christianity—the triune oneness of God the Father, Son, and Holy Spirit and the miracle of the incarnation of Christ. At the apex of heaven, an overwhelmed Dante is granted a glimpse of the countenance of the Lord, "the love that moves the sun and other stars."

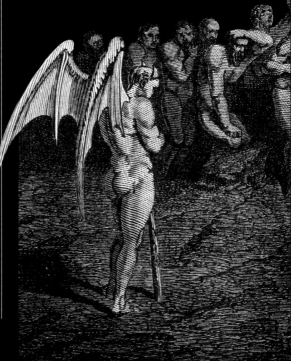

The grim boatman Charon (foreground) ferries damned souls across the river Acheron to begin their eternal torment in the inferno. Among those suffering there are hoarders and squanderers (background), who sinned through greed. They are doomed forever to roll massive boulders against each other. At right, Dante and Virgil see the lustful, who were carried away by passions in life, now perpetually tossed and whirled in hurricane winds. Among the famous lovers are Cleopatra, Helen of Troy, and Helen's lover, Paris.

Condemned like all heretics to spend eternity in a burning grave, an old enemy of Dante's rises to ask the poets for news of his son on earth. Souls in hell remember the past and see dimly into the future, he explains, but they have no sense of the present in the world of the living. Fiery tombs of the heretics litter a vast plain within the walled city of Dis in nether hell. In the lower depths is found the forest of suicides (far right). There, the souls of those warped by the sin of self-murder are transformed into grotesque trees. Because they rejected life on earth, they now stand fixed and withered in hell.

In the sixth circle of hell, Virgil and Dante observe the simoniacs (left), faithless priests who used their position in the church to gain temporal wealth. During life, they reversed the proper order of things by placing earthly gifts above the gifts of God. Thus they are condemned to spend eternity upside down in reeking holes. The sixth circle is divided into ten trenches. In the seventh of these (above), monstrous snakes sting and crush the souls of thieves. In a lower trench (below), sowers of discord among families, churches, and nations are doomed to be continually split apart by a sword-wielding demon. Their cuts heal only to be reopened.

The giant Antaeus (above), who in Greek mythology represented pride and primitive emotion, lowers Virgil and Dante onto the frozen lake that fills the pit of hell. There, beneath nether hell's fires, lies the silent, eternally frozen Lake Cocytus (right), which holds the souls of traitors to country and betrayers of family.

In the icy pit at the bottom of hell, Virgil and Dante stand in fear and awe on a high cliff as they watch the brooding Devil chew on the head of the archtraitor Judas Iscariot. Other treacherous souls are scattered across the frozen waste below.

As the poets travel through purgatory, they see fresh souls arriving in the company of an angel (below). Relying as he often did on Greek myth to convey his Christian message, Dante placed in this afterworld Arachne (bottom), a woman who was transformed into a spider by the goddess Athena for the sin of pride. An expert weaver, Arachne had challenged Athena, whose purview included crafts, to a weaving contest. Athena wove into her web stories of those who angered the gods, while Arachne chose to include examples of the gods' errors. The prideful mortal's reward was to lose both the contest and her human form. At right are passionate souls that, though good and true in life, must be purged and tempered by purgatory's flames.

A kindly spirit (above, top) helps Dante across Lethe, the river separating purgatory from paradise. Its waters blot out all memory of sin. In heaven, the poet finds souls of the blessed (above, bottom). Doré exercises artistic license with these beings, making them appear more angelic than human. The artist takes more liberties as Dante and Beatrice stand at heaven's apex (right), where souls circle God's blinding, divine light. In Dante's vision, souls here had shed their bodies and become pure radiance, shining forms of love and goodwill.

The Soul and the Séance

ames Kidd's money at work: The year was 1973. In a Psychical Research Foundation laboratory at Duke University, two gray-striped kittens padded nervously inside a wooden box eighty inches long, thirty inches wide, and ten inches deep. The floor of the box was a grid whose numbered squares called up the incongruous image of a shuffleboard. The kittens were called Spirit and Soul, but their behavior belied the serenity of their names. The box was unfamiliar and potentially threatening, as was the human who sat nearby and peered at them. So the kittens roamed warily, all the while mewing their distress.

About a quarter of a mile away in another campus lab was the kittens' owner, a Duke undergraduate named Keith Harary who would, in time, go on to a notable career as a parapsychologist. On this day, he was an experimental subject for other scientists. He lay on a couch, his body wired to an array of equipment that measured, among other things, his heart rate, respiration, and brain waves. If all went well, he would soon pay a reassuring visit to his cats. But he would not leave the couch to do it. By his own account, Harary was a veteran of out-of-body experiences—OBEs, in parapsychology parlance—in which his consciousness slipped its fleshly moorings and voyaged, disembodied and unencumbered, wherever it would.

In their lab, the kittens still paced. Robert Morris, a Ph.D. in biological psychology and the PRF's research coordinator, tried to keep up with their movements. His job was to log their progress along the grid's numbered squares, but the felines' nervous stalking made this difficult. Morris lifted Soul out of the box, leaving Spirit alone. The remaining kitten continued to patrol the grid and cry. Then it stopped. Its constant mewing gave way to total silence. It moved to a corner of the box, curled up, and appeared calm, all signs of alarm gone.

Spirit's period of quietude coincided with an apparent OBE by Harary— a time during which certain changes were noted in the student's body. Instruments registered increasing relaxation, oddly coupled with rising heart rate and respiration that normally indicate not relaxation, but arousal. The OBE over, Harary's first reaction was to condole with the other experiment-

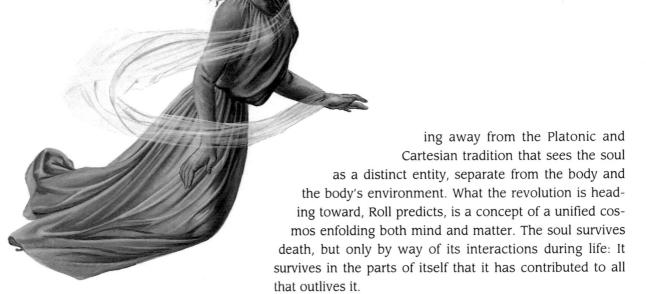

ers about what he assumed had been a failure. He understood he was to visit both kittens, he said, but during his astral trip—an early one in a series—he saw only Spirit.

Years later, PRF founder William G. Roll, who oversaw the Duke project that was funded by part of the PRF's portion of Kidd's legacy, recalled the work with Harary and Spirit. He was cautious, saying only that "results suggested that the animal responded to something." To a detachable soul? To a spirit capable of leaving the body during life and perhaps after death? Like diligent psychical researchers before him, Professor Roll shies away from such sweeping conclusions. He himself does not believe in the existence of a soul as a personal and discrete entity that can permanently separate from the body.

"The survival question is so colored by presuppositions about what humans are and what might survive death," Roll says. "The question has generally been cast in Cartesian terms of mind-body dualism [pages 51-55]. But this is being increasingly questioned." In fact, Roll reports, a quiet revolution is underway in parapsychology, one lead-

ing away from the Platonic and Cartesian tradition that sees the soul as a distinct entity, separate from the body and the body's environment. What the revolution is heading toward, Roll predicts, is a concept of a unified cosmos enfolding both mind and matter. The soul survives death, but only by way of its interactions during life: It survives in the parts of itself that it has contributed to all that outlives it.

According to the parapsychologist, the rethinking of the most basic questions in survival research is largely responsible for the lack of conspicuous activity in the field in recent decades. New ideas are being formulated; the testing must come later. If the root concept of the new thinking proves promising—if the soul seems indeed to be some impersonal part of a cosmic continuum—surely much work will go into proving it, for the very idea kicks aside the underpinnings of traditional psychic investigation. During the heyday of such research—a time roughly spanning the last two decades of the nineteenth century and the first two of the twentieth—the working hypothesis hinged on the soul's particularity and individuality. Many of the field's founders, deeply influenced by traditional Christian notions about the soul, saw it as a purely spiritual entity, separable from the body, capable of surviving and bearing intact the essence of personality.

So thinking, they sought the soul through evidence, such as it was, that certain individual personalities survived death. The search's venue in those days was more apt to be a séance room than a laboratory. Much attention was devoted to mediums, who purportedly spoke for the dead or allowed the dead to speak through them. In addition, inves-

tigators studied cases of purported obsession or possession, in which spirits of the dead seemed to invade personalities of the living. Those who came to believe in evidence of the soul's survival were called survivalists.

These old pursuits have not vanished. Even as new ideas are proposed and pondered, many modern parapsychologists continue to visit mediums, to investigate hauntings and apparitions, to study and comment on decades-old cases in hopes of unearthing new truths. But the efforts have diminished. Arrant fraud among mediums discouraged many researchers. Others were put off by the anecdotal nature characterizing much of the best survival evidence and the inability to make that evidence conform to the empirical standards of science. Still others were disheartened by the persistent failure, despite years of honest effort, to produce concrete, controllable, repeatable results. And lacking such results, funding for parapsychology projects has grown ever more scarce.

But while tantalizingly inconclusive, hints of the soul's survival as brought to light by psychic research have almost always been intriguing. Consider, for instance, the case of a certain craftsman who found himself inexplicably transformed into an artist.

By the winter of 1907, Frederic L. Thompson feared for his sanity, so thoroughly had a powerful obsession come to dominate his life. Plagued by hallucinations and on the verge of destroying his career as a goldsmith in New York City, he appealed to a friend for advice. The friend directed Thompson to Professor James H. Hyslop, a former instructor in logic and ethics at Columbia University and executive head of the American Society for Psychical Research. At

Promising evidence of life after death, a large sign identifies a Spiritualist church in London. The smaller sign advertises a "special evening of clairvoyance," at which, supposedly, a medium will communicate with the dead. A belief in discarnate spirits is the core of Spiritualism, whose churches, numerous in the nineteenth century, are rare today.

their first meeting, on January 16, the distraught Thompson told the professor that his troubles had begun about eighteen months earlier, in the summer of 1905, when he was unaccountably overwhelmed by an urge to sketch and to paint in oils. Not particularly interested in art and without any formal training, Thompson nevertheless felt himself compelled to draw and paint. Even the subjects he depicted seemed to be imposed on him and not his own choices.

Thompson had a startling explanation for his predicament: He was convinced, he told Hyslop, that he was under the mental sway of Robert Swain Gifford, a landscape painter of some distinction. Thompson claimed to have met Gifford briefly on a few occasions, but, the craftsman said, he knew nothing of the artist's work. How or why Gifford could exert such control over him Thompson could not imagine, but the conviction persisted. Then, in 1906, Thompson went to see a Gifford exhibit at a New York art gallery, only to learn the artist had died the preceding summer. The death had occurred at virtually the same time that Thompson had first been driven to paint. As Thompson was trying to digest this astonishing coincidence, he heard a voice that seemed to issue from a painting on the gallery wall: "You see what I have done. Can you not take up and finish my work?"

From that time on, Thompson told Hyslop, he began to have frequent visual and auditory hallucinations and to feel more driven than ever. Always something of a dreamer, he now had constant difficulty holding on to reality. When he sat down to work at his trade, he would often drift off into a trancelike state, awakening hours later to discover a painting that he had no memory of producing. Although Thompson's artistic gifts fell well short of Gifford's, his skill increased over the months. He actually sold several paintings, and people remarked on their similarity to Gifford's work.

Hyslop's first reaction was that Thompson was, indeed, demented. But as an investigator of psychic phenomena, Hyslop considered the possibility that Thompson's contact with a discarnate spirit might be real. Psychologist William James had proposed that insanity is in some instances attributable to spirit possession, and this possibility

A Semimaterial World

French educator Hippolyte Rivail (below) was dubious of the Spiritualist movement sweeping America and Europe in the 1850s. The idea that the spirits of the dead could communicate with the living seemed unlikely to Rivail—until he attended his first séance. Not long after that event, he renamed himself Allan Kardec, supposedly at the suggestion of the spirits, and formulated his own philosophy, which he called Spiritism.

Kardec maintained that spirits, though incorporeal, are made up of an actual substance differing from ordinary matter in that it cannot be perceived by the five senses of sight, hearing, smell, taste, and touch. In life, spirit is united to the body by means of an intermediary material that Kardec referred to as the perispirit—a substance roughly equivalent to the Spiritualists' ectoplasm. At death, the union of spirit, perispirit, and body is sundered, and only spirit remains, to await reincarnation.

Spiritism today survives mainly in Brazil, where, often combined with African religions and indigenous Indian faiths, it claims believers numbering in the millions.

occurred to Hyslop after hearing Thompson's bizarre story.

Hyslop took Thompson to a number of reputable mediums, introducing his companion as Mr. Smith and giving no clues about his alleged problem. Theoretically, if Thompson had simply been hallucinating, the séances would turn up nothing suggesting postmortem contact. But just two days after Thompson's first visit to him, Hyslop hit what seemed to be pay dirt: A medium reported seeing behind Thompson the figure of a man who was fond of painting.

In March, the pair traveled to Boston for a session with a renowned trance medium, Mrs. Chenoweth. During the session, her control spirit, Sunbeam, seemed to speak for and about Gifford (although she did not name him), describing his clothes and mannerisms, the favorite themes and colors of his paintings, and even a rug in his house. Gifford reportedly promised Thompson through Sunbeam, "I will help you, because I want someone who can catch the inspiration of these things as I did, to carry on my work."

With Hyslop's blessing, Thompson set out to visit places Gifford had frequented. The first stop was a visit with Gifford's widow at their Nonquitt, Massachusetts, summerhouse. There, Thompson reported that he saw a painting whose subject and composition closely resembled one of the sketches Gifford had directed him to draw. From Nonquitt, Thompson traveled to Gifford's birthplace on Naushon Island off of Cape Cod. Again, he found scenes he claimed matched those he had seen in visions and had painted. In what must have been a riveting moment, Thompson heard a voice directing him to a particular tree. On its trunk were carved Gifford's initials and the year 1902.

On his return to New York, Thompson's mental state began to improve; it appeared that the trip and the séances he attended under Hyslop's guidance were therapeutic. If the spirit was not exorcised, neither was it as troublesome as it had been, and it grew even less so with a climactic event that occurred during a séance in December of 1908.

Oddly enough, the spirit seemed to have a coy preference for anonymity. It revealed itself as Gifford in many ways, but in the almost three years that it dominated Thompson's life, it declined to identify itself by name. Then, at the fateful December séance, it purportedly directed the hand of the medium to write the initials RSG—Robert Swain Gifford. After that, communications began to fade. Confirmation of the spirit's identity was perhaps all that the goldsmith needed to regain his equilibrium, for he and Hyslop parted ways soon after. Even so, Thompson still claimed some spiritual contact with Gifford into the 1920s. Moreover, Thompson abandoned his old work. He found he now enjoyed painting, and he had some talent, for he was eventually inducted into the prestigious Salmagundi Club, whose members were all professional painters. As late as 1922, his works were being shown in a New York gallery.

Hyslop was convinced Thompson was possessed, but over the years other psychical researchers have demurred from that interpretation of the classic case. Contemporary British psychologist Alan Gauld thinks a more likely explanation lies with what parapsychologists call Thompson's super-ESP—a powerful compound of telepathy, clairvoyance, precognition, and retrocognition. According to this hypothesis, gifted individuals can extend their paranormal senses to events, objects, and states of mind far more numerous, obscure, and distant in time and space than might seem possible. Gauld believes that Thompson's brief acquaintance with Gifford could somehow have triggered a powerful unconscious extrasensory link. After years of unwitting telepathic and clairvoyant scavenging in Gifford's internal and external worlds, Thompson had acquired a great deal of information about the artist. Steeped as he was in another man's life, it was easy for Thompson to believe that he was acting under the direction of Gifford's spirit. Nevertheless, Gauld posits, it is far more probable that Thompson's own mind, with its store of memories acquired by ESP, was the critical factor. The experience was not proof of a soul's survival.

But Gauld's hypothesis, by his own admission, pre-

sents problems. Thompson's unconscious motive for taking on another man's identity is not clear. Certainly, the experience was a frightening and financially costly one. Nor does Gauld think that clairvoyance or even psychokinesis satisfactorily explains how Thompson learned to paint so well in such a short time. Despite these shortcomings of the ESP hypothesis, however, Gauld finds it sounder than the possession theory for the Thompson-Gifford case.

On the other hand, possession seemed to several parapsychologists the most obvious interpretation of the Watseka Wonder case reported in 1879 by physician and firsthand observer E. Winchester Stevens. At the focus of the incident were two young women, Mary Roff and Lurancy Vennum. Born in 1847, Mary had lived for a time in the little town of Watseka, Illinois. The recollections of friends and family suggest that she may have been clairvoyant, since she was reportedly able to read closed books and sealed letters. After years of suffering periodic seizures that she said were brought on by "a lump of pain in the head," Mary died on July 5, 1865.

Twelve years later, thirteen-year-old Lurancy Vennum, who lived with her family near Watseka, began to suffer fits and trances. Mary Roff's father heard about Lurancy and, perhaps sympathetic because of his late daughter's similar problems, paid a visit to the Vennums. He had had a nodding acquaintance with the family six years earlier, when the Vennums had lived next door for a few months.

Mr. Roff suggested to the worried parents that they allow his friend Dr. Stevens to examine Lurancy. They gratefully agreed and on January 31, 1878, Dr. Stevens, accompanied by Roff, arrived to find Lurancy apparently possessed. She seemed to submit alternately to the personalities of a sullen old woman and a sorrowful young man.

Trying to release the girl from this state, Dr. Stevens hypnotized her and, according to his published report, he "was soon in full and free communication with the sane and happy mind of Lurancy Vennum herself." Neither "sane" nor "happy" seems quite apt, since the entranced girl told the doctor of an angel that wanted to come to her in place of the "evil spirits" attempting to control her. Asked who the angel was, Lurancy replied, "Mary Roff."

By the following day, Lurancy Vennum had succumbed entirely to the personality of Mary and claimed to be homesick for Mary's family. When Mrs. Roff and her married daughter, Minerva Alter, heard of this development, they set out to see the Vennum girl, whom they had reportedly never met when the Vennums were their neighbors. At their approach, Stevens wrote, Lurancy "exclaimed exultingly, 'There comes my ma and sister Nervie'—the name by which Mary used to call Mrs. Alter in girlhood. As they came into the house she caught them around their necks, wept and cried for joy, and seemed so happy to meet them. From this time on she seemed more homesick than before. At times she seemed almost frantic to go home."

After a week of deliberation, the Vennums agreed to let Lurancy live with the Roffs for a time. The girl showed an astonishing familiarity with the events of Mary's life. On one occasion, for instance, she reminded Mrs. Alter of an incident from many years before. Pointing to a spot in the backyard, she said, "Right over there by the currant bushes is where cousin Allie greased the chicken's eye." Mrs. Alter recalled the peculiar incident very well, remembering their taking the chicken into the house for first aid. It seemed to the Roffs the kind of recollection that no one could come up with by chance. They were convinced that their dead Mary had returned to live again in Lurancy's body.

But no such accommodation was permanently in the offing. Almost as suddenly as it had seemed possessed, Lurancy's old personality reasserted itself, and three months and ten days after she had gone to live with the Roffs, she returned to the Vennums. On occasion, however, when she visited the Roffs, she briefly reverted to the Mary persona.

Alan Gauld, one of modern parapsychology's most notable theorists, is uncertain whether Lurancy was indeed possessed by Mary. He suggests that Lurancy could have been a medium and Mary the control spirit (an entity said to guide or sometimes possess—but only temporarily and with consent—a medium), although cases are rarely reported in which the control manifests itself for so long. Taking a non-survivalist tack, the late Frederick C. Dommeyer, a professor of philosophy at San Jose State College in California and a frequent writer on paranormal topics, proposed that Lurancy Vennum obtained such thorough familiarity with

Mary Roff through ESP that she could impersonate her.

Since cases of apparent possession invite multiple interpretations, they have not provided compelling evidence for the soul's survival. More persuasive to some investigators are incidents that point to a well-defined purpose in a spirit's communicating with the living and to a resemblance between the supposed spirit and the person it claims to have been in life. Such cases are thought to be all the more convincing if the spirit's message seems beyond the intellectual capacity of the medium or mediums through whom it is delivered. One of the most persuasive of all such cases involved several luminaries—some living, some dead—who helped pioneer psychical research in the nineteenth century. It was known as the Lethe case, and it even had some elements of an experiment, since the living participants carefully plotted their encounter with the dead.

The central figure of the Lethe case was the late Frederic W. H. Myers, a classicist at Cambridge University and a leading light of the SPR until his death in 1901. The question of the soul's survival after death had haunted him. After he died, several mediums reported receiving messages from a spirit claiming to be Myers. How to verify this claim absorbed Myers's colleagues, among them George B. Dorr, vice-president of the ASPR. It occurred to Dorr that he could pose a classical literary question to Myers through the Boston medium Leonora Piper. The puzzle seemed a useful investigative tool, since neither Dorr nor Piper was versed in the classics, effectively ruling out their supplying a solution, advertently or inadvertently. And if Myers had in fact survived death and was trying to communicate with colleagues and friends, he would have both the motive and the knowledge to come up with an answer containing convincing indications of his intellect and character.

On March 23, 1908, Dorr sat with an entranced Mrs. Piper, ready to write down any responses she detected. The investigator directed a question to Myers: "What does the word Lethe suggest to you?" It was a tricky reference. Lethe, Greek mythology's river of forgetfulness in the underworld, has been a literary allusion down to the twentieth century, so a spirit could have chosen among thousands of writers or literary works in his answer.

The responses that Mrs. Piper received in the first sitting and several more that followed baffled Dorr. There were many classical references, but they were so fragmentary and obscure as to seem impenetrable. Unsure whether they related to Lethe at all, Dorr sent the scripts to British

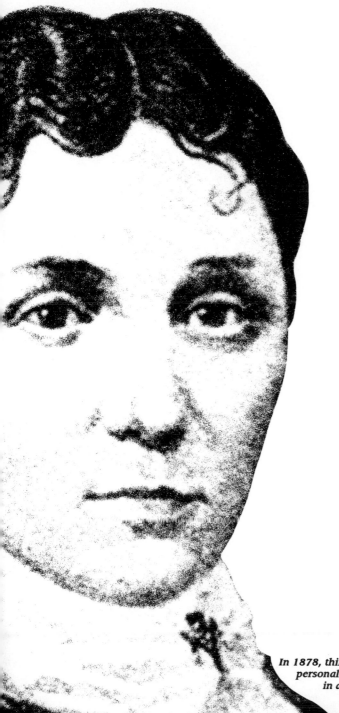

In 1878, thirteen-year-old Lurancy Vennum (near left) assumed the personality of the late Mary Roff (center left) for several months in an ostensible case of spirit possession known as the Watseka Wonder —so named after the town where both girls lived. In her role as Mary, Lurancy stayed with the Roffs for several months in their house (far left), where she reportedly behaved as if she truly were Mary Roff's spirit incarnate.

classicist and psychical investigator James G. Piddington. He, in turn, discovered a passage in the Latin poet Ovid's *Metamorphoses* that he believed explained most of the fragments that Mrs. Piper had received. Lethe figured in the story of the drowning of a king named Ceyx and the transformation of him and his queen, Alcyone, into birds. It was not a particularly well-known passage, nor were Ceyx and Alcyone prominent figures in classical mythology. Thus Piddington concluded that only a scholar thoroughly familiar with *Metamorphoses* could possibly have come up with such a reference. Moreover, the tone of the scripts evoked Piddington's old friend. If Myers's mind was not involved, Piddington wrote, it was a mind "which deliberately and artistically imitated his mental characteristics."

Piddington and Dorr were now certain Myers had proved his survival in responding to the literary puzzle. Other psychical researchers were encouraged but not wholly convinced. Cambridge physicist Sir Oliver Lodge thought more evidence, in the form of cross-correspondences, was needed to validate Dorr's test. Cross-correspondences are messages received by different mediums that are unintelligible or ambiguous when read individually but, when examined as a whole, are rife with meaning.

For researchers seeking evidence of survival, cross-correspondences help rule out alternate explanations. The mediums who participate often live in different places and are not known to communicate with each other through normal sensory channels, so collusion in fakery is difficult. Super-ESP becomes an unlikely explanation, since the process would be fantastically complicated for two or more mediums unknown to one another to obtain knowledge from people living or dead, communicate it to one another telepathically, and evolve disparate fragments of information that could later be melded into a unified whole.

In his quest for cross-correspondences in the Myers case, Lodge asked the help of an English automatist medium (one whose purported spirit communications take the form of writing) known by the pseudonym Mrs. Willett. A woman of high social standing and reputedly impeccable virtue, Mrs. Willett had produced several scripts alleged to contain evidence of Frederic Myers's survival. Besides her apparent receptivity to messages from him, Mrs. Willett's ignorance on two scores—Myers's alleged communications to Piper and the classics—recommended her to Lodge as a collaborator on the case. On February 4, 1910, the medium opened a sealed envelope containing a note signed by Lodge. It read, "My Dear Myers, I want to ask you a question—not an idle one. WHAT DOES THE WORD LETHE SUGGEST TO YOU? It may be that you will choose to answer piece-meal and at leisure. There is no hurry about it."

M rs. Willett's results were everything Lodge had hoped for. By his interpretation, the medium's scripts were suffused with Myers's personality, his classical erudition, and his humor. There was even a pun on Dorr's name, which was to Lodge's mind a very telling bit of evidence. Mrs. Willett could not have known it, but the living Myers had been addicted to puns. One of the responses even suggested that Myers understood why the Lethe question had been posed a second time: "That I have to use different scribes means that I must show different aspects of thought, underlying which unity is to be found," wrote the spirit Myers. Lodge described Mrs. Willett's scripts as "supplementary to, and by no means identical with, those obtained through Mrs. Piper. They contain a common element, and in my judgment are characteristic of the same personality."

To Lodge, the cross-correspondences were so rich that he felt they justified a momentous conclusion: The surviving personality of Frederic W. H. Myers had been in touch with his old friends through Mrs. Piper and Mrs. Willett. Lodge reminded his colleagues that "in science we are not unused to discoveries of considerable magnitude; and if, after due scrutiny facts become compulsory, men of science must be ready to enlarge their scheme of the universe so as to admit them."

Contemporary psychologist Gardner Murphy, a past president of the ASPR and one of parapsychology's most respected investigators, is forced to the same conclusion. Though wary of any broad statements about the soul's survival, Murphy finds in the Myers scripts so much autonomy, intent, cogency, and individuality that "the case looks like communication with the deceased." Alan Gauld concurs, rejecting super-ESP as a plausible explanation. (Many parapsychologists find the Lethe case all the more convincing in light of the role apparently played by the discarnate Myers in a much larger body of scripts known as the SPR Cross-Correspondences. As their uppercase designation implies, the Cross-Correspondences, which involved as many as ten mediums working for more than thirty years to produce thousands of pages of scripts, are considered by the

psychic-research community to be definitive examples of this type of evidence of the soul's survival.)

Although Alan Gauld ruled out super-ESP in the Lethe case, he does think it has sometimes deluded mediums and sitters into believing themselves in touch with spirits when they are not. He points to a 1922 case in which a voice claiming to be an old school chum named Gordon Davis spoke to British mathematician and parapsychologist Samuel Soal through Blanche Cooper, a direct-voice medium. Soal believed Davis had been killed during World War I, and when the voice answered his question about this point ambiguously, Soal interpreted the response to mean Davis was dead. The voice, which reminded Soal of the way his friend had spoken, mentioned several details from their shared past that Soal knew were accurate. In two later sittings, a control of Mrs. Cooper's described in detail a house in which Davis's wife and child were said to live. Three years later, Soal was startled to hear Davis was alive. He and his family lived in a house virtually identical to the one that had been described to Soal previously. To the parapsychologist's amazement, the Davises had not moved into the house until a year after the sittings with Mrs. Cooper.

The case can be explained if Mrs. Cooper exercised two or three types of ESP. According to Gauld, she might have telepathically gleaned information about Davis from Soal, then located the living Davis and done more probing from afar. Her information about Davis's house could be attributed to precognitive telepathy—Davis was a real-estate agent and might have known about the house long before deciding to live there. She might also have made a clairvoyant excursion to flesh out her knowledge of it.

However they are explained, most cases claiming contact with spirits of the dead have a common thread—some previous life relationship, however tenuous, between the communicating soul and the living recipient of the message. Far rarer are what parapsychologists call drop-in contacts, which seem to be random encounters. In these cases, a communicator who is ostensibly unknown to either the medium or the sitters and has no prior claim on their minds arrives uninvited at a séance.

In the fall of 1937, for instance, an unknown spirit barged in while two Icelanders, voice medium Hafsteinn Bjornsson and sitter Einar Kvaran, were holding one of their frequent séances. When Kvaran asked its name, the alleged spirit, speaking through Bjornsson, refused to reveal it, saying, "What the hell does it matter to you what my name is?" The spirit, obviously male, said he had come looking for his leg. At subsequent sittings, he continued to demand that the sitters produce it, much to their bafflement, since the prickly intruder would not explain his peculiar demand.

After fish merchant Ludvik Gudmundsson began to attend the sittings, the irascible spirit claimed that his leg was in Gudmundsson's house. Astonished by this assertion, Gudmundsson declined any effort to find and return the

missing limb until he knew who the communicator was. The spirit then identified himself as Runolfur Runolfsson and said that on October 16, 1879, he had gotten drunk, fallen asleep on the beach, and been swept out to sea. The tide bore his body back to the beach, where dogs dismembered it. His remains were discovered and buried the following January, but a thigh bone was missing. It washed back up later and, after being passed about among townsfolk as a curiosity, wound up in Gudmundsson's house.

Part of the tale was verified in records at Utskalar church, which was, as the voice had said, the site of Runolfsson's grave. Oldtimers whom Gudmundsson questioned vaguely remembered something about a thigh bone being found, and a man who had lived in his house years before said a carpenter had placed such a bone between the inner and outer walls of one room. Gudmundsson tore out the wall and found a long thigh bone. If it was Runolfsson's, it supported his claim that he had been tall. Gudmundsson arranged a Christian burial for the bone at Utskalar, complete with a sermon and a reception. Bjornsson did not attend, but he held a séance after the ceremony. The voice thought to be Runolfsson's spoke, describing the event down to the cakes served and thanking Gudmundsson.

lthough the alleged Runolfsson had achieved his goal, he continued to communicate through Bjornsson. In 1972, when the medium attended an ASPR meeeting in New York, Runolfsson made several séance appearances. Witnessing one of them was Ian Stevenson, a professor of psychiatry at the University of Virginia and a leader in survival research. Stevenson was prompted to visit Iceland, where he interviewed two dozen people familiar with the case and reviewed historical documents containing information about Runolfsson. Stevenson concluded that, despite some indications that Bjornsson might have been getting part of his information from the Icelandic Archives, the case contained compelling evidence for survival. He noted

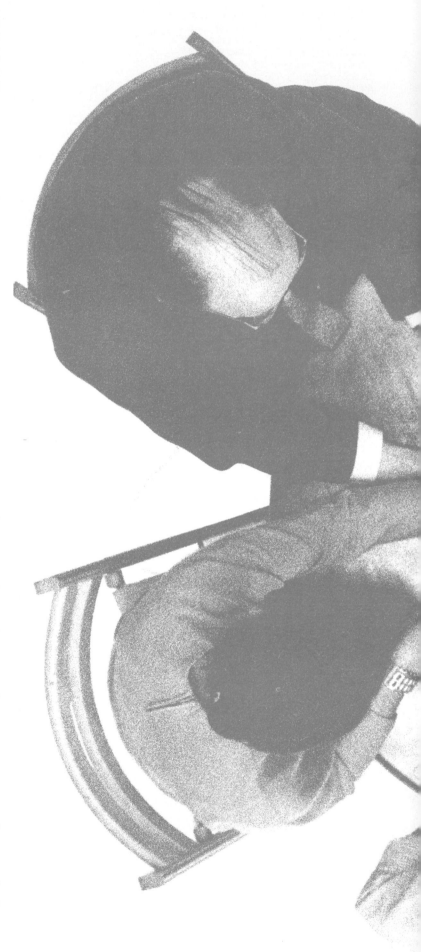

that neither the medium nor any other living person was likely to have the wealth of detail that emerged about an obscure man who had been dead sixty years. It also seemed implausible that Bjornsson could invent and dramatize convincingly such a vivid and idiosyncratic personality.

Drop-in communicators such as Runolfur Runolfsson are, according to investigator Alan Gauld, more likely to make themselves known at amateur séances than at those of professional mediums. He speculates that it is harder to interrupt a professional concentrating on contact with a chosen communicator. If a drop-in does get through, a professional has less reason than a curious amateur to welcome random contacts and to do research in public records and other sources to verify the strangers' statements.

And often there are not many clues to go on. Runolfsson, it is claimed, hung around for years, but drop-ins are more likely to talk and run, as Ian Stevenson has remarked. One such case that Stevenson studied focused on the spirit of a Frenchman killed in World War I. The dead soldier allegedly turned up several times in late 1932 and early 1933 at the weekly séances of housekeeper and medium Mme B. Bricout and M. Jacques Brossy, a retired businessman living in St. Etienne. By Brossy's account, the affair began at a time when he and Bricout were using a Ouija board to seek the surviving spirits of their dead spouses. By way of the board, a presence that Brossy believed to be a frequent spirit communicator named Juliette offered to relay messages from a spirit unknown to either the medium or her sitter. If Brossy could verify the statements of this new entity, his belief in the spirits would be bolstered.

The communicator's name, Juliette reported, was Robert Marie. Before dying a soldier's death in 1914, he had lived in the Norman town of Villers-sur-Mer, where his father was caretaker of a large villa. Robert said that his young son, also named Robert, had contracted a case of meningitis that left him deaf and mute. At times the soldier was bitter about his own death and his widow's remarriage.

Almost immediately, Brossy wrote to the notary of Villers-sur-Mer for any record of Robert Marie. The notary

wrote back that the man had been married and was the father of a child and had died at the battle of the Marne in 1914. Brossy also located Robert Marie's mother, but she declined to answer any of his questions.

aving done what he could to verify the communications, Brossy let the matter rest for almost three decades. Then in 1963, he wrote a letter about his experience to Stevenson, who by that time had won an international reputation for psychic investigation. Stevenson visited Brossy and Bricout later that year and launched his own probe of Marie's life. Some of Brossy's research was confirmed, but there were several important contradictions. Five informants whom Stevenson questioned, including Robert Marie's sister-in-law, insisted that little Robert was the son of Louis Ferdinand Marie, the brother of Robert Marie. Louis had also been killed in World War I, at the battle of Verdun in 1916. The sources also denied that Robert Marie had ever married. Stevenson speculates that the Villers-sur-Mer notary had simply been mistaken about Robert Marie's marriage and parenthood (an honest mistake is understandable, since Stevenson's informants told him that the soldier, whose given name was August Charles Robert Julien, was called Charles by his family and friends). Another possibility Stevenson raises is that Robert was not married but had fathered an illegitimate son who was adopted by Louis Ferdinand and his wife. Intent on hiding this family secret, the informants denied the truth of the boy's paternity. Whoever the father was, Stevenson concludes that the details revealed in the séances must refer to one or both of the Marie brothers and no one else in the world, principally because they were the only Villers-sur-Mer residents named Marie to die in the war.

Some of the confusion may have arisen from the dead, not the living. Stevenson remarks that if both brothers were attempting to communicate through Juliette, they could have interfered with each other's messages. Alternatively,

Juliette's transmittal could have been imperfect. Stevenson writes, "In the present case I believe that one or both of the Marie brothers, surviving death, influenced the communication, but could not guide it sufficiently to achieve complete accuracy." Survival seems to Stevenson the only viable explanation for the case, despite its factual inaccuracies.

When the statements that supposed spirits make can be verified in public records or by living persons, the evidence for survival is usually considered strongest. For this reason, some investigators find especially persuasive a case with a hauntingly beautiful name—Swan on a Black Sea. In this much-chronicled case, a purported spirit shared detailed memories that were validated by the living.

The woman who was apparently so successful in tapping into a stream of memory was automatist Geraldine Cummins. A successful playwright and novelist as well as a medium, Cummins received a letter at her home in Ireland in August of 1957 from W. H. Salter, an official of the SPR in England. He explained that an SPR member whose mother had died the previous year wished "to give her an opportunity of sending him a message." The son was hoping for proof that his mother's soul had survived. Salter hinted that time was of the essence: "By the end of the year the evidential significance of the case will probably have declined through the publication of some facts at present known only to very few persons."

What Salter did not tell Cummins explicitly was that the person the SPR member hoped to reach had been active in psychic circles but had used a pseudonym to keep her identity secret. Salter himself was the author of the forthcoming article he had alluded to, in which the targeted spirit's real name would be revealed. With that information public, it would be harder to defend any apparent contact against antisurvivalist charges of fraud. The less a medium could possibly know, the better the evidence would be. For that same reason, Salter had been careful to choose a medium from a different country who, as far as he knew, was not acquainted with friends or relations of the mother.

Cummins agreed to undertake the assignment. Salter

Of Human Wisdom

Claiming to draw from his own mystical experiences, philosopher Rudolf Steiner developed his first theory of the soul while he was still a schoolboy. Born in Austria in 1861, the youth postulated that everyone had what he called a soul space—a sort of inner stage for the activities of a mysterious spirit world—which existed just as surely as physical space.

As he matured, Steiner's mystical bent deepened. In 1902, he became the general secretary of the German branch of the Theosophical Society, a quasi-religious organization whose doctrines—including a belief in reincarnation—borrowed heavily from Eastern mysticism. But from the beginning Steiner had some ideological differences with the Theosophists. For one thing, he refused to accept as true anything that he had not personally experienced through his own spiritual

searching. In 1913, he broke from the society to establish a vehicle for his own personal philosophy, which he called Anthroposophy—"human wisdom"—perhaps to differentiate his views from those of Theosophy, which means "divine wisdom." It was Steiner's belief that spiritual knowledge should not be the esoteric property of a select few, but a goal common to all

humanity. "In every man," he said, "faculties lie dormant by the exercise of which he can gain knowledge of the higher spheres."

The existence of higher spheres was a keystone of the Anthroposophical Society, which Steiner founded on the basis of insights that he claimed to have received clairvoyantly. He proposed that humans belong simultaneously to three interacting spheres: the body to the physical world; the soul to the intellectual; and the spirit to a higher spiritual realm. The body lives and dies according to natural laws, Anthroposophy held, but the spirit is eternal and subject to reincarnation. The soul, which lives only in the present, links body and spirit during one's lifetime. Moreover, the soul is ruled by the law of karma, which holds that the thoughts and actions during one incarnation determine an individual's fate in the next: "The impressions that the soul receives, the desires that are satisfied, the joys and sorrows that it experiences," Steiner wrote, "depend on its actions in previous incarnations." Repeated lives on earth give humans the opportunity to awaken their inherent faculty for spiritual knowledge through such pursuits as meditation and the study of the natural sciences. The ultimate goal of these disciplines is spiritual perfection.

Before his death in 1925, Steiner had applied his philosophy to a number of fields, including education, architecture, and the arts. His four so-called mystery plays, which follow the successive incarnations of a group of spiritual pilgrims as they make their way toward higher knowledge, convey in dramatic form the basic concepts of Anthroposophy.

Rudolf Steiner (above) designed a special seal for the cover of each of his mystery plays, including this one for The Soul's Awakening. In it, a snake swallowing its tail—an ancient symbol of eternity—encircles a sunburst that represents the soul.

told her only that her "absent sitter" was Major Henry Tennant, a name she said meant nothing to her. On August 28, she directed "Astor," her regular spirit guide, to make contact with Tennant's mother. In a trance, Cummins transcribed Astor's words: "I see her as a very old woman in the eighties, very fragile. She lost a son when he was . . . nineteen or twenty, I think. I see the memory of that agonizing news. It is like a scar on the mind. . . . She has another very dear son. It is a middle-aged man, early forties." The day after the first séance, there was a second, during which the old lady, who called herself Win, revealed through Astor that from childhood on she had had the gift of automatic writing and was now anxious to get a message through about the psychic work she had done in life. The message Cummins wrote out was for W. H. Salter: "I lift my ban entirely. That is to say, I trust you absolutely. You have a free hand. Publish what you like." Astor reported that Win had two companions that day—a frail old scholar, Gerald, and Francis, a young man who had died in a sporting accident in a foreign country. There seemed to be a special bond between the three spirits, one Astor did not understand.

It was becoming clear to Cummins that Win and her two spirit companions had been important members of the psychic community. In a fourth séance on September 22, Astor reported that Gerald "is the leader of a Group and wishes to seize this opportunity to use . . . Winifred, as a kind of liaison officer in several brief communications." Two days later, Cummins learned that the group was composed of the spirits of people who had lived in Cambridge and formed the core of the early SPR. Gerald could only be Gerald, Lord Balfour, once a leader of the Cambridge Group. Win, or Winifred, Cummins guessed, must be Mrs. Willett, famed for her work in the SPR Cross-Correspondences.

This discovery supposedly did not open up new sources of information for Cummins about Mrs. Coombe-Tennant's personal life, since she had so determinedly kept it private even as her mediumistic skills had won notice for "Mrs. Willett." Nevertheless, after only six sittings, Cummins had apparently learned many intimate details, for

Art and the Aeon

All the vogue among many artists of the the late nineteenth century, Theosophy held a special lure for the visionary Irish poet, essayist, and painter AE Russell. He was introduced to the mystical creed as a young man in Dublin by a fellow art student named William Butler Yeats, who would go on to become one of the greatest modern poets. Yeats would also remain Russell's lifelong friend.

Russell must have found Theosophy's doctrines of reincarnation and karma particularly appealing, corresponding as they did to his own earliest musings about the soul and its fate. When he was only sixteen, Russell claimed, he had become "aware of a mysterious life quickening within mine. It was no angelic thing but a being stained with the dust of travel, having myriads of memories and a sacred wisdom."

Born George William Russell in 1867, the artist became AE through a printer's error. He signed one of his early works *Aeon,* a word that supposedly came to him unbidden, and the printer deciphered it as AE. When Russell later discovered the word had mystic meaning—it signified a being emanated from God—he adopted the diphthong as his pseudonym. Thereafter it symbolized for him his immortal soul, passing from body to body on its mission of purifying itself.

In both his painting and verse, Russell sought to express his vision of the soul's nature. The preface to his first book of poems, *Homeward: Songs by the Way,* reveals his faith in reincarnation and his longing for his soul's ultimate return to a heavenly perfection that was its source: "I moved among men and places, and in living I learned the truth at last. I know I am a spirit, and that I went forth in old time from the Self-ancestral to labours yet unaccomplished; but filled ever and again with homesickness, I made these songs by the way."

Russell denied that his belief in Theosophy rested on blind faith. Rather, he said, its conclusions merely confirmed his own insights, achieved through the arduous

The experience of the soul in various phases of reincarnation appears to be the subject of the highly symbolic mural below, painted by AE Russell (inset) around 1892 on the walls of the Dublin lodge of the Theosophical Society. Russell lived there as a member about seven years, thriving on the daily companionship of fellow spiritual seekers.

search for his own soul. This spiritual quest led him to some novel embellishments on familiar mystical themes. For example, he developed a rather comforting view of karma that revolved around what he called the law of spiritual gravitation. He believed that fate recognizes affinity, continually drawing together groups of loved ones as they travel from life to life so that they might pursue their spiritual adventures collectively. Thus Russell could reassure himself that he would never lose the friends, such as Yeats, whom he valued so deeply.

Also characteristic of Russell was the intense form of concentration he called retrospective meditation. Every night, he visualized the events of the day, then the preceding one, then the ones before that, images rolling back like a movie in reverse. He claimed that with practice he could see back to his infancy, and in time even further, breaking loose from his present incarnation to glimpse past ones. He said he had lived in ninth-century Spain, in ancient Egypt, and more than once in Gaelic Ireland—in some lives male, and in others female.

Russell believed every human soul chose of its own free will to leave its heavenly station and enter the cycle of birth, death, and rebirth. Only this way could it gain the experience that would make it richer than before its descent: ''They are but the slaves of light / Who have never known the gloom. / And between the dark and bright, / Willed in freedom their own doom.''

W. H. Salter, after reading the scripts, traveled to Ireland to confirm that ''Mrs. Willett'' was, as Cummins had guessed, Winifred Coombe-Tennant. The comments on family lore and history, gossip about friends and relatives, allusions to the activities of the Cambridge Group, childhood memories, recollections of Henry and the death of his brother Christopher in World War I rang so true to Henry Tennant that he did not believe Cummins could have known them from any source other than his mother. In script five, for instance, the communicator quoted a line from William Butler Yeats that Tennant recognized as one of his mother's favorites. On other occasions, the discarnate entity reminisced about her half sisters from her father's first marriage, her grandfather's house in Wales, and her service as a magistrate. She discussed the marital troubles of Myers, who had been unhappily married to her sister-in-law Eveleen Tennant. The young Francis alluded to in the séances was Gerald Balfour's brother, who died in a mountain-climbing accident in Switzerland.

Despite all the scripts' rich detail, some statements seemed fragmentary or opaque to Henry Tennant. In the fourth script, for example, the communicator's closing words were, "Confusion, can't hold on. But Swan rests on a black sea. . . ." Henry hazarded that this was a reference, not too significant, to Swansea, a town near the birthplace of his Welsh grandmother. But to Geraldine Cummins, the fragment symbolized the very soul of Winifred Coombe-Tennant, rising like a swan above the black sea of death.

Henry avowed that, despite occasional lapses, his mother's personality shone in script after script. C. D. Broad, a member of the English SPR establishment and reluctant survivalist who has analyzed the Cummins—Coombe-Tennant scripts—forty in all—concludes that the communicator consistently speaks in the voice of a strong-willed grande dame who displays an interesting mix of upper-class haughtiness, political radicalism, maternal devotion, and mysticism that her friends would surely recognize. In Broad's opinion, the "single, self-consistent, outstanding personality" implied by the communications makes it hard to doubt their authenticity.

More telling is Broad's judgment of the factual content of the scripts. In the foreword to Cummins's book *Swan on a Black Sea,* he points out that it is crucial to determine what proportion of statements in the scripts are both factual and especially relevant to the ostensible spirit communicator. "In marked contrast to the contents of many mediumistic utterances, they are not in the least vague, general, allusive, or oracular," Broad notes of the scripts. "They abound in extremely concrete detail about named persons and places, and about definite events in which these were concerned. Moreover, of the large mass of concrete testable state-

ments, very nearly all are true, and when a mistake in detail is made . . . it is nearly always corrected in a later script."

Only a paranormal phenomenon, Broad asserts, can explain the enormous amount of information in the first six scripts, which are more credible than later ones as they were transcribed before W. H. Salter's article about Mrs. Willett was published. The details Mrs. Coombe-Tennant's stream of memory offered up to Cummins would seem beyond the reach of Salter and Major Tennant—supposedly Cummins's only living contacts in the case. This fact leads Broad to reject telepathy as a possible avenue to this information. Clairvoyance is also ruled out, since no printed materials recorded Mrs. Coombe-Tennant's life so extensively.

road writes that "much the simplest and most plausible hypothesis prima facie is that Mrs. Coombe-Tennant, or some part or some aspect of her, survived the death of her body . . . and that she from time to time controlled, directly or indirectly, the pen of the Automatist G.C." The scripts, Broad proposes, owe their unusual richness to the fact that Mrs. Coombe-Tennant, a medium herself in life, knew "the ropes very much better than the average surviving spirit, in regard to communicating through a medium."

But even a survivalist such as Broad stops short of declaring that the scripts irrefutably prove the soul's continuation after death. Rather, cases such as Swan on a Black Sea and Lethe are merely suggestive. The evidence they contain is at best anecdotal and not empirical. Ian Stevenson, another survivalist, would like to develop a more rigorous scientific approach to survival research. He suggests, for instance, that controlled experiments in drop-in communications would produce far more reliable information and weaken the possibility of mediumistic fraud.

Among parapsychologists, many opponents of the survivalist hypothesis believe in the reality of other psychic phenomena, such as telepathy and clairvoyance, which are by no means universally accepted themselves. Still, to the minds of these investigators, psychic talents provide the most rational explanations for apparent cases of survival. One science-minded doubter who devoted years to studying the paranormal was the late E. R. Dodds, professor of Greek at Oxford University. He was a leading proponent of the super-ESP hypothesis. Although Broad and others argue that the soul's survival is the simplest explanation of cross-correspondences and similarly intriguing cases, Dodds countered that this explanation involves a complex combination of unproven hypotheses. Besides assuming that personalities continue to exist after bodily death, the survivalist position assumes that they retain an accurate memory of their past lives and continue to be aware of events occurring among the living. Survivalism also assumes that discarnate beings can reach the minds of the living and communicate with them, either by possessing the medium or telepathically influencing the subconscious mind. By comparision, the super-ESP hypothesis is simplicity itself.

South African psychical investigator J. H. M. Whiteman, a professor of theoretical mathematics at the University of Capetown, contends that a certain intellectual murkiness underlies the difficulties facing survival research. The problem, Whiteman says, "seems to be the fact that we are hoping to deduce the survival of something whose nature we are unable to specify clearly. If it is the personality which is claimed to survive, what exactly is a personality apart from the body? . . . For an investigation of survival to be possible, we must have at least a preliminary rough idea of what survival could be."

Professor W. G. Roll, who oversaw the Duke experiments involving kittens and OBEs, is one parapsychologist who believes he has a workable notion of what survival—and the soul—may be. Roll ascribes to an Iroquois Indian concept called the long body. According to the Iroquois, the long body is all that has impinged upon us or been impinged upon during life. There is no true line of demarcation between the self, the self's environment, and other selves. Each of us interacts with others and with the place we inhabit in the world. We become part of others, and they of us. There is no distinction between self and other. Similarly, there is no distinction between ourselves and the ground we walk on or the air we breathe. When we die, what survives us is our long body. We persist as part of a continuum that, by extension, takes in all the universe.

Roll believes this idea is central to parapsychology's revolution in the making, a movement that will turn away from Theosophical and philosophical ideas about individual souls and veer toward ideas shared by modern physics. As Roll notes, quantum physics *(pages 130-139)* posits a world in which the usual distinctions between consciousness and matter, the observer and the observed, begin to blur.

Moreover, the parapsychologist speculates, this redefining of the soul could have beneficial moral implications. "The world has progressively gotten away from us," he says. "First we believed the earth was flat with heaven above and hell below. Then we thought it was round and floating in space, but still the center of the universe. Then the sun became the center, and then there was no center. Now we are refocusing on the human psyche as the center. We see that the self is individual and also universal. Each self and its body has a place and a time in the world, and each self is connected to everything that exists. The self lives and dies and at the same time transcends birth and death. Traditional science has focused on the self as an entity, separate from the rest of the world. Modern science, including parapsychology, sees the self as the center of relationships that extend beyond our usual image of the body and its limitations. The self connects us, in both the receptive mode and the creative mode, to other people and things, although they may seem remote in time and space. When we become aware of this matrix of connections, the self is experienced as the other, and separations of time and distance fall away." In such a construct, Roll suggests, the soul in life creates its own legacy, its own fate, in what it shares of itself with all around it. "It is good that we are pulling heaven and hell into ourselves," he says. "Now we are responsible for the world."

Art from the Other Side

Here we do not eat at all, the spirit is sustained by mental food. . . . We are able to choose our own surroundings. . . . We have time for everything, . . . there is none of that striving after wealth and none of the show and haste that we had in the earth life. . . . We are bodies of light."

Thus was the afterlife described by one of its inhabitants—at least according to London artist Ethel Le Rossignol. The daughter of a prominent Channel Islands family, Le Rossignol was a well-regarded painter with an interest in Spiritualism. In February 1920, she was trying her hand at automatic writing, the process in which souls of the dead supposedly commune with the living by inspiring a human host to write their messages. Suddenly her pencil drew a caricature of a dead friend, a man she identified only as JPF, who told her that, "having passed the barriers of death, he still lived."

For the next thirteen years, Le Rossignol later related, her deceased friend kept in regular touch, guiding her to describe and illustrate the spirit world. Among the resulting drawings and paintings was the work reproduced above, a symbol-laden rendering of twelve intertwined spirits that represent the hereafter's "great companionship of shared unity."

Exhibited in 1929 by the London Spiritual Alliance and later collected in book form, the pictures still fascinate to this day. Although examples of automatic writing abound, spirit art is rare, and Le Rossignol's pictures are unusual both in their vision and in their voluminous detail.

"The Winter I spent in Egypt was my last Winter on earth," read one message that Ethel Le Rossignol claimed to have received from her dead interlocutor. Writing of the night his earthly body died, JPF told of falling asleep, tired and ill. When he woke up, he was outside of his body, viewing it as if it were still slumbering in bed. "I willed at first with all my strength to get back into my body but I could not do so, and saw it being carried off and put into a grave at Luxor. That was *astonishing* and I could not believe that I was what the World calls dead."

Happily, JPF soon learned that "what the World calls dead" was merely the beginning of a new and infinitely richer life than the one he had left behind. He assured Le Rossignol that she need not grieve for him, then began briskly directing her how to render his new existence in pictures.

The first was a pencil sketch (*below, left*) of the "spirit house" where the souls of the newly dead arrive from earth. Often still weak from the illnesses or injuries that killed them, they are greeted by loving, comforting spirits in a vaulted hall with huge windows, through which streams the bright "light of wisdom."

The spirit house is located in what JPF calls the Astral Sphere, the first stage of a new soul's journey through the spirit world. In the Astral Sphere, the neophytes recuperate and begin preparing to advance higher. Progress hinges largely on the souls' gaining wisdom and thus growing "more and more in goodness and truth," explains JPF.

In pursuit of wisdom, they engage in pleasant mental exercises such as contemplating beautiful objects or studying music, art, and science. In a drawing called *The Power of Thought (below, right)*, souls practice a kind of astral architecture, erecting a house by mental power alone. The chastely nude figures are seen willing different parts of the building into existence from the whorls forming in their hands.

Once souls have advanced to the first of the higher levels, the Spiritual Sphere, they begin rising through the increasingly lofty spheres of wisdom, harmony, love, and holiness. An "aspirant" spirit may now serve as a kind of conduit ("a channel of inspiration," as JPF puts it) between the higher spheres to which he aspires and the earth. The painting at near right depicts an aspirant rising above a triangle that contains the impure, passion-ridden human beings who inhabit the physical world. The aspirant connects the wretched humans with the larger figures of highly evolved spirits called messengers, whose words of wisdom issue from their mouths in multicolored ribbons.

In a related picture (*far right*), a more advanced aspirant carries an emblem called the arrow of purpose, which parts the darkness for the souls below him.

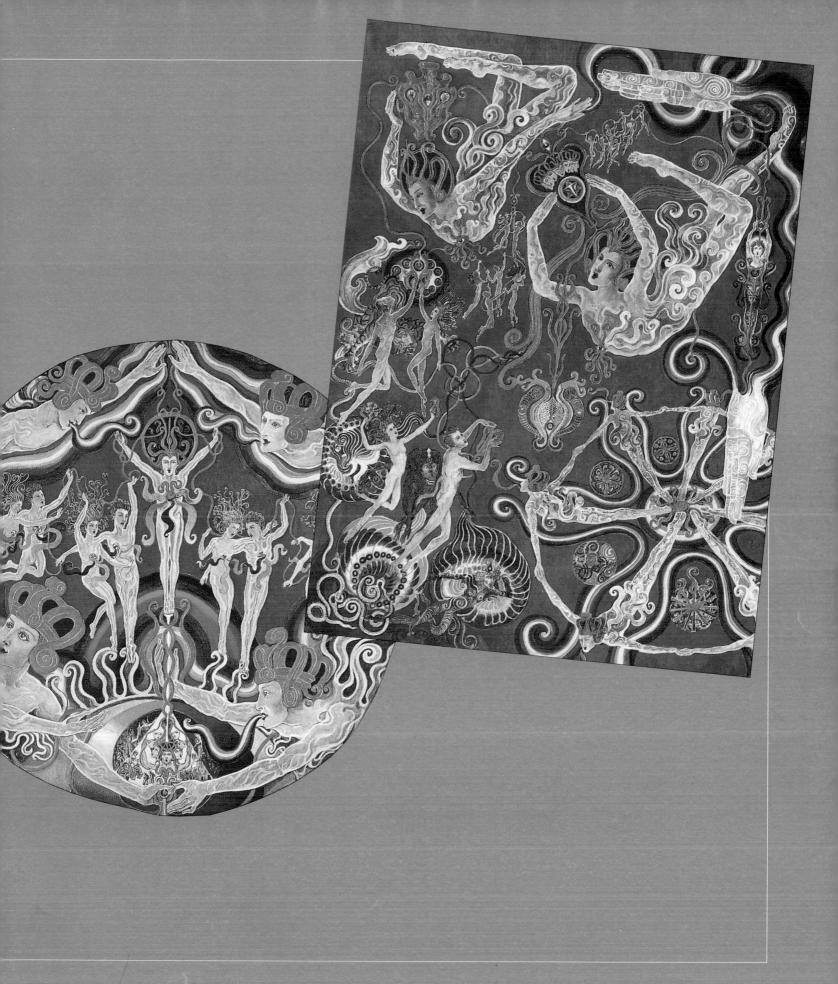

Over the years, Ethel Le Rossignol's collaboration with JPF produced increasingly exotic art. The four pictures here seem almost oriental in their jewel-like colors and intricate, highly stylized composition. (In fact, anyone skeptical of Le Rossignol's claims of spirit guidance might note that she once studied under Frank Brangwyn, a prominent artist known for his love of oriental decorative art and for his own sumptuous, colorful works.)

By the time she painted these final pictures, Le Rossignol's symbolism had become impenetrable, and her spectral guide's lengthy comments on it shed little light. His early, beguiling descriptions of a paradise peopled with luminous souls had given way to bizarre ramblings. Referring to the top painting, opposite, JPF points out a Christ figure in the twelve-pointed star, then writes obscurely: "The NINE entering REALITY-IN-OPERATION is thus the crucial at-one-ment."

Despite the demented tone of such observations, the enigmatic works Le Rossignol finished in the early 1930s as her contact with JPF began waning still reflected the basic concept of the afterlife that was evident a decade earlier—a view of all life joined within a great continuum where spirits of the dead help and inspire spirits of the living, and humans still on earth can savor hopes of immortality and perfection.

Possessors of the Orb (above, left) depicts the fruitfulness of divine love. Love and creativity radiate from a master spirit and are relayed to an earthly family by spirits possessing "the Orb of Creative Wisdom." Another painting illustrating the beneficence of the disembodied *(above, right)* shows guardian spirits protecting and sustaining earthly creation, represented by a man using a spade and a woman caring for her children. *Consummation (opposite, bottom),* the last of Le Rossignol's forty-two spirit works, stresses a theme of unity by incorporating all the symbolic elements of the preceeding pictures under the outstretched arms of the master. The ultimate goal of aspirant spirits is to become one with this omnipotent presence.

The 1929 London Spiritual Alliance exhibition of the spirit pictures stirred such interest that the show, planned for ten days, was extended for three months. Thereafter, however, the works attracted little attention. Le Rossignol's supposed contact with JPF ended in 1933, and under her married name, Ethel Beresford Riley, she painted pictures of flowers.

In 1958, her brother privately published the spirit art in a book called *A Goodly Company.* "Look what Ethel has brought out!" he announced as he presented the book to his relatives. Family members agreed that it was a handsome volume, but none of them expressed much interest in it, and neither did the world at large.

When Le Rossignol died in 1970, she willed the art to a companion named Mrs. Summers, to "deal with according to her known wishes." Whatever those wishes were, they subsequently died with Mrs. Summers, and the paintings wound up in the London College of Psychic Studies. There they remain today, curious artifacts offering a comforting—if not verifiably accurate—portrayal of life in the hereafter.

CHAPTER 4

Science and the Soul

ithin a small private room in a London hospital, a lean, normally energetic man spends his days playing solitaire and scribbling his thoughts in a diary. His name is Clive Wearing, and he is an authority on Renaissance music. But he will never learn more about that subject or any other. In 1985, he suffered a severe bout of viral encephalitis. The disease destroyed an area of his brain called the hippocampus, whose function is to store memory. His intellect is substantially intact, and he can retrieve parts of his life from before the illness; he knows and loves his wife, for instance, and he still plays the piano. But his immediate past is closed to him. Perceptions flit through a slit in time no more than two minutes wide, and then they vanish. Each handful of minutes erases the minutes before. Nothing registers, nothing sticks.

Wearing's wife, Deborah, enters the room, and he jumps up to embrace her. "How are you, where have you been all this time?" he demands. There is a breathlessness, an urgency to the greeting, as though she has been lost to him for ages. The terrible truth is that Deborah saw him that very morning, and he has already forgotten. She points to the jottings in his diary, where he noted the visit, but the words only puzzle him. "That wasn't me," he insists. "I didn't write those things."

Stripped of every memory almost before it forms, a vital center of his brain destroyed, Wearing lives trapped in each moment, his soul held hostage to a perpetual, ephemeral present that has neither antecedent nor outcome. Since our sense of ourselves is derived in part from the sum of our previous experiences, what is the state of Wearing's soul? Is it diminished? Does it still exist?

The pursuit of the soul, once laughable to followers of Western rationalist tradition, is now occupying some of the best minds in contemporary mainstream science. Of course, these days few scientists or philosophers call their object of study the *soul;* the word is too fraught with mystical and religious overtones. Rather, they refer to *mind* or *consciousness* or *personality.* Whatever the terminology, however, the quest is unchanged. Its object remains the very essence of what it means to be human. Thus in medical clinics and dissecting rooms, in physics labs and psychology labs, at engi-

neering schools and computer design shops, researchers in specialties ranging from microbiology to astrophysics are addressing the issue. What is human consciousness, and where does it reside? Is it confined to the intricate folds and chambers of the brain, to the electrical discharge of the several billion crackling neurons and synaptic connectors that constitute our gray matter? Or is it more than that?

Various laboratory experiments, and the very nature of thought itself, suggest to some observers that consciousness may extend far beyond the physical brain, that it may waft through time and space to influence events in ways that have very little to do with ordinary notions of cause and effect. And if this much is true, if consciousness somehow exists outside the boundaries of currently known natural law, is there a chance that it may survive the death of the brain itself?

Among the first modern scientists to ponder these questions were Sigmund Freud, the father of psychoanalysis, and his disciple Carl Jung. Freud's theory of the unconscious mind, with its seething conflicts and unruly sexual urges, had already rocked the medical profession when the two men first met in 1907. His three-part division of the psyche—the passion-driven id, the rational ego, the moralistic superego—flew in the face of prevailing dogma. Nor did his methods of investigation, through word association

and the careful analysis of his patients' dreams, carry much weight at first. But Jung was fascinated. He, too, thought dream analysis would open the door to a hidden mental landscape, one even more sweeping perhaps than what Freud envisioned. A lively correspondence developed between the two men.

Within a few years the friendship began to fray, however. One point of contention was their differing views of paranormal phenomena, including what would later come to be called extrasensory perception, or ESP. Freud was a doubter, a materialist impatient with anything he could not prove by scientific means. But Jung, the son of a clergyman, came from a family of mystics. His cousin held séances, his mother kept a diary of her premonitions, and he himself reported experiencing moments of terrifying psychic intensity. As a child he saw visions of God, and later he would dream the deaths of relatives—often at the very instant they expired, he said. Once, in 1913, he was seized by an overpowering spectacle of Europe "covered with a sea that turned to blood" and in which corpses floated. A year later, most of Europe was at war.

The disagreement between the two great psychoanalysts lurched into the open while Jung was visiting his mentor in Vienna in 1909. During a conversation one day, he asked Freud about his attitude toward precognition—the

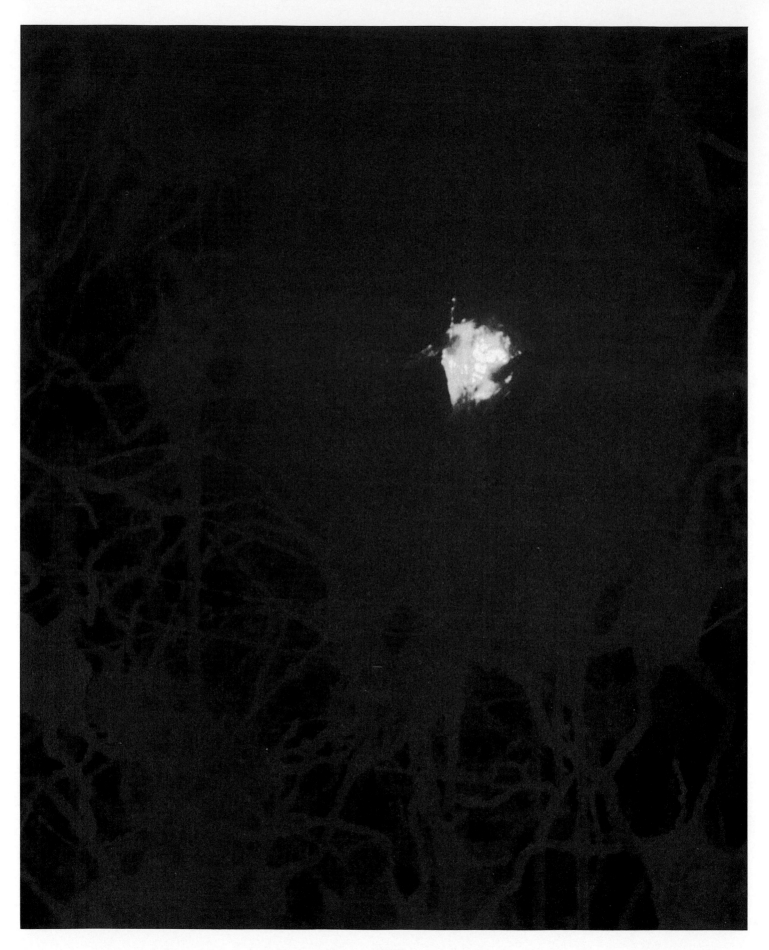

power to foresee the future. Freud, sober and patrician, dismissed the idea as so much nonsense—a reflection, Jung later wrote, of his "materialistic prejudices." But as Freud continued talking, the younger man felt an odd sensation, as though his diaphragm had turned to red-hot iron. Suddenly there was a loud crack, like a rifle shot, in the bookcase next to them.

"There is an example of a so-called catalytic exteriorization phenomenon," Jung announced, referring to the theory that emotional agitation could occasion poltergeist-like effects.

"Oh, come," Freud responded, "that is sheer bosh."

"You are mistaken, Herr Professor. And to prove my point I now predict there will be another such report."

Again the bookcase detonated—much to Freud's amazement. Similar raps occurred in the days that followed. Still, Freud remained unconvinced. "The furniture stands before me spiritless and dead," he later wrote in a letter to Jung, "like Nature, silent and godless before the poet, after the passing of the gods of Greece."

So the lines were drawn. It was the same age-old conflict that had troubled thoughtful minds since the days of Plato and Aristotle—the philosophical materialists on one hand, trusting logic and observation alone, the idealists on the other, open to larger influences. Now the discussion had entered the rarefied domain of the brain sciences, psychology and neurology.

Freud continued to refine his portrait of the human psyche, drawing on his clinical work with patients suffering from hysteria and tying it to dissecting-room studies he had made in medical school. The brain, he decided, can be likened to an electrical mechanism with an elaborate network of wires and switches connecting its various parts. The "nervous excitation" of his patients was no more than a "quantity of current flowing through a system of neurons."

Few of Freud's contemporaries took exception to this basic scheme; it was the standard model, and it remains so today. An outside stimulus, experienced by the senses, sends electrical impulses coursing through the brain's channels, causing reflex actions in the muscles. Some impulses become imprinted on the brain cells as memories, and they may remain there as part of the unconscious. But whenever an impulse reaches the cerebral cortex—the brain's upper portion, near the top of the skull—it takes the form of conscious thought. Freud equated the cortex region with the ego, the faculty of self-awareness. If he thought there was more to consciousness than that—some less mechanistic component of mind that might equate with a soul—he never said so in print.

Jung followed his own path, exploring the implications of his dreams and visions. Beneath each individual's conscious thoughts, and beyond the subconscious region that supports them, there lies, Jung postulated, an even more basic reality. It takes the form of a vast, free-floating continuum of myth and archetype that is shared by all humankind. This collective unconscious, as Jung termed it, operates outside the boundaries of time and space and is largely hidden from rational interpretation. But it is a realm of great power and potential. It may surface in moments of artistic creation or religious ecstasy—and also, perhaps, in the form of precognition or other psychic experience.

The majority of people, caught up in the prevailing rationalist dogma—"the disease of our time," Jung called it—shun or deny such manifestations. But they do so at their own risk. Far better, Jung advised, to reach down into the universal psychic ocean and discover what it holds. The rewards might be rich beyond measure: a profound sense of unity and purpose or an archetypal image that unites the seeker with his true psyche.

Most of today's scientific community, it must be said, subscribe to the more prosaic views of Freud and the materialists. Ever since the Enlightenment raised rationalism as truth's only standard, physical science has generally marched forward according to clearly defined rules of cause and effect: Whenever a force or stimulus is applied to the system under study, all other things being equal, a predictable result will occur. When researchers examine the workings of the brain, they proceed according to the same logic.

Thus surgeons and anatomists apply their scalpels to the cerebral cavities of operating-room patients and laboratory animals. Neurobiologists pore over paper-thin slides of tissue on microscope slides. Geneticists study heredity's bearing on the brain, biochemists chart the effects of drugs and enzymes, electrical specialists spend countless hours wiring the skulls of their subjects into EEG machines and analyzing the graph-paper squiggles that result. Lab rats are sent through mazes, mice are fed diets of caffeine and cocaine, songbirds are schooled by computers, chimpanzees are surgically altered to deprive them of memory. And in all this activity a basic premise dominates: The brain is in essence a machine, a kind of biological watch that ticks away in a predetermined manner. Its entire functioning—including its conscious awareness of its own existence—is evaluated in terms of biology, physics, and chemistry. The renowned British biologist T. H. Huxley set down the ground rules more than a century ago. "All states of consciousness . . . are immediately caused by molecular changes of the brain structure," he declared. He then went on to draw the logical conclusion: "We are conscious automata, . . . parts of the great series of causes and effects, which, in unbroken continuity, composes that which is, and has been, and shall be—the sum of existence."

The rationalist approach has produced some astonishing results, for the brain has been revealed as the most complex, highly developed entity that we know. Indeed, whatever we know resides within it. Every impression of our senses, every pang and desire, every word and idea from the prose on this page to the loftiest constructions of science and philosophy, by definition filters through it. This huge capacity is miniaturized into a sphere of pinkish-gray flesh the consistency of rice pudding, which weighs about three pounds and fits comfortably into the palm of a hand. Within it is lodged a virtually unimaginable concentration of brain cells—neurons, as many as 100 billion by some estimates—each one connected by thousands of microscopic fibers to neighboring neurons. The current fashion is to compare these junctures to the wiring of a sophisticated computer. But a computer would have to be complex indeed to approximate the human brain's capacity or rival its

The Essence of Life

What exactly is life? What distinguishes the living from the inanimate? For millenniums, philosophers and scientists have struggled to pinpoint the subtle something the living have and the lifeless do not. Some have said life emerges from nonlife, arising from combinations of inanimate matter. In this view, a human is only an arrangement of chemical compounds. None of the constituent chemicals is alive by itself, but once they join in the right configuration, nothing else—no immaterial essence—is needed to constitute life.

One proponent of this theory was William Harvey, the renowned English physician who applied the concepts of mechanics in his analysis of body processes. Harvey revolutionized anatomical science in 1628 by showing that the heart is a pump circulating blood. Although blood was regarded as a magic fluid by many of his contemporaries, Harvey placed it in the realm of natural law.

In later years, however, Harvey seemed to modify his mechanistic stance while pursuing the theory that humans, like other vertebrates, develop from eggs. As he tried to understand embryonic development, he came to attribute the process to some type of life power or internal force.

Over the next three centuries, a number of respected scientists would embrace the idea of such a life force, rejecting the view that human life is basically mechanical. They subscribed to a doctrine called vitalism, which contends that there is a vital power intimately involved with, but distinct from, the physical matter composing living creatures. Aristotle called this force psyche; over time, it has been known by other names, among them the demiurge, the entelechy, and the soul.

George Ernst Stahl, a German physician and chemist who lived from 1660 to 1734, believed the soul was immaterial and beyond the reach of physical science. The soul controlled the body, he thought, and knew how to care for it and cure its ills. Nineteenth-century English naturalist Alfred Russel Wallace also insisted there was more to human life than could be learned from physical studies alone. A friend of Charles Darwin, Wallace arrived independently at his own theory of evolution. But, disturbed by his findings, Wallace exempted the human spirit from the evolutionary scheme. He posited that human consciousness was a special creation biology could not account for.

Regarded by some as the greatest vitalist since Aristotle, twentieth-century German scholar Hans Adolf Eduard Driesch began as a biologist, but his search for the essence of life led him to philosophy. Convinced that a subtle power animates living matter, Driesch drew on biological experiments and abstract reasoning to make his case that the functioning of living creatures cannot be explained solely by the chemical properties of their bodies.

Driesch died in 1941, but the vitalism debate rages on. Neither science nor philosophy has established conclusively what life is, or whether its definition requires the concept of a nonphysical dimension.

electrical and biochemical intricacies, many of which are as yet unplumbed.

Clearly no one will soon chart the brain's wiring system in all its minute detail. But researchers have been able to map out various areas within the brain that seem to control special functions. A section in the back receives signals from the eyes via the optic nerve. Other regions trigger various emotional states and sensations of hunger, thirst, pain, sleepiness, and sexuality. One key structure is the hypothalamus, an interior section near the top of the spinal cord. The hypothalamus apparently has several vital tasks. A scalpel thrust into one tiny portion will cause a lab animal to stop eating. Another thrust, and he will feast himself to death. An electric shock to the hypothalamus, in an animal or a human, will bring on a convulsion of rage or terror.

Is there also a spot within the brain that houses our conscious mind, as Freud suggested? A group of master cells that tells us who we are and unites us to the larger world of thought and spirit? This question took on new urgency several decades ago because of a controversial breakthrough in medicine. A Los Angeles brain surgeon named Joseph Bogen, working with psychobiologist Roger Sperry from the University of California, developed a radical technique for treating severe epilepsy.

An epileptic seizure is caused by the chaotic firing of a cluster of neurons—a lightning storm in the brain, so to speak—and in the worst cases the lightning bounces back and forth between the brain's two hemispheres. So Bogen and Sperry tried severing the cable of tissue that connects the hemispheres.

The operation brought much welcome relief, but it also had some puzzling side effects. Most patients, on recovery, appeared to be perfectly normal. They could read, write, cook dinner, converse, and make decisions pretty much like everyone else. But when Sperry subjected them to a series of psychological tests, certain lapses appeared.

Each side of the brain, it seems, has charge of specific functions. The left hemisphere "sees" images conveyed from the right eye

Over a span of nearly three hundred years, the question of whether life originates with physical forces alone or involves some vital essence consumed four great scientists and philosophers: (from top) physician William Harvey, chemist George Ernst Stahl, naturalist Alfred Russel Wallace, and biologist Hans Adolf Eduard Driesch.

*A Nobel laureate and pioneer in split-brain research,
Roger Sperry contends that human consciousness is something
more than its physical source, the brain.*

and controls movement on the right side of the body. In most people, the left hemisphere is also the center for reading, speech, mathematics, and logical analysis. Conversely, the right hemisphere is wired into the left eye and controls movement on the body's left side. It tends to be visual rather than verbal and seems to operate more by intuition than logic. Normally, the two halves communicate without effort. But in split-brain patients the dialogue breaks down, particularly in matters of language.

If a picture of a horse is flashed in front of a patient's right eye, for example, he has no difficulty pronouncing it a horse. The image registers on his left, or verbal, hemisphere. When the same picture is flashed to the patient's left eye, however, he remains speechless. He cannot describe what he has seen, and in many cases he thinks he has seen nothing. But—and here is the most peculiar part—he is perfectly capable of sketching the horse, using his left hand. Then a quick glance at the sketch enables him to make the verbal connection.

 ven though the right brain is inarticulate, it may still have its own unstated thoughts. In one famous experiment, Sperry screened a left-eye image of a nude pinup. His split-brain subject, a young woman, giggled and blushed, although she could not explain why, since her right brain could not form words for what she was seeing with her left eye. Some part of her mind understood that it ought to be embarrassed, even if it was not able to articulate the reason.

Where, then, does consciousness reside? Could there in fact be two different kinds of consciousness, one vocal and analytic, the other silent and subjective, each lodged in its own hemisphere? This seems to be the case with split-brain patients, and perhaps it is true for the rest of us as well. So thinks neurosurgeon Bogen, at any rate. "Pending further evidence," he declares, "I believe that each of us has two minds in one person."

Another interpretation is reached by neurologist Michael Gazzaniga of Cornell University, a former student of Sperry's. Gazzaniga ran some split-brain experiments of his own. One of his subjects was a woman in her thirties named Vicki, who after her operation had some nasty residual problems, beginning with the business of getting dressed in the morning. "I would open my closet, get ready to take out what I wanted, and my other hand would just take control," she reported. Her left hand was the maverick. Receiving instructions from her right brain, it usually selected an entirely different costume from the one she consciously intended. Eventually, Vicki learned to subdue it, establishing discipline in her right hemisphere. What is more, the same hemisphere, normally silent, began to acquire a rudimentary gift of gab. It made mistakes, to be sure, but clearly Vicki's verbal abilities are no longer entirely independent and localized.

From this and other experiments, Gazzaniga concluded that we have a multitude of conscious selves, not merely two, and that they are distributed in scores of different minicircuits throughout the brain. "The mind is not a psychological entity but a sociological entity," he writes, "being composed of many submental systems."

Sperry himself, whose split-brain research earned him a Nobel prize, takes an even broader view. Consciousness, he believes, is not confined to any specific chunk of gray matter. Rather, it is a glorious composite, the sum of all the brain's parts working together. Just as billions of years ago some complex protein molecules clumped together in the world's primordial oceans and so produced life, each person's nerve cells, buzzing away in electromagnetic harmony, give rise to something greater than themselves. A new entity emerges, at a higher level of evolutionary development. Though based on physical processes, it belongs entirely to a world of cerebral abstraction and is subject to its own particular laws.

With human thought thus raised to a higher level, the gates swing open on a wider avenue of speculation—extending, perhaps, toward the timeless and incorporeal

Lost in Eternal Thought

The notion of eternal life and survival of the soul could take on a new meaning in the twenty-first century if some computer wizards have their way. A number of researchers in computer science are daring to dream of creating immortality in the laboratory. These scientists foresee a day in the not-too-distant future when human beings will be able to preserve their minds forever by discarding that frail package of flesh, the brain, in favor of computer-program consciousness.

According to experts, the transferring, or downloading, of a human mind and personality into a high-tech habitation would begin with precise, section-by-section mapping of the brain. Then computer programs would be designed to duplicate the operations of each group of neurons. In theory, the sum of these programs would be the functional equivalent of the brain they copied. The programs would constitute a computerized model containing all the memories, desires, dreams, ideas, and other elements that make a person unique. Encoded on a tape, disk, or other appropriate medium, this software replica of the brain could be duplicated to create numerous backup copies for insurance in case of damage to the original. After the death of the physical body and brain, the computerized version of the mind could live forever in a succession of robot bodies.

Among those expressing enthusiasm for this brand of eternal life is artifical-intelligence pioneer Marvin Minsky of the Massachusetts Institute of Technology. "I think it would be a great thing to do," he says. "I've spent a long time learning things, and I'd hate to see it all go away."

But what implications would such technology hold for the soul? If, as some believe, the soul equates to human consciousness, perhaps the human essence could find itself imprisoned in a robotic shell with a magnetic memory.

world of spirit. To be sure, Sperry is a scientist of the old school, a staunch materialist. Sperry's theory, like the conjectures of his associates, still supposes that the brain is a machine and that such abstract qualities as mind and self-awareness are simply the result of its smooth and invisible functioning. As another researcher phrases it, "The mind is a process of the brain."

Some scientists vehemently disagree, however. Sir John Carew Eccles is one of the grand old men of neuroscience, winner of the 1963 Nobel prize in medicine for his pioneering work on synapses, the connecting points between brain cells. And although Eccles concurs that the brain is machinelike in its operation, he regards the mind as something entirely different.

Eccles arrived at this conclusion by reviewing a series of experiments on the cerebral cortex, the area that controls most higher forms of mental activity. Part of the cortex, for example, commands the movements of our bodies by sending signals to our arms and legs. Furthermore, within the cortex is a special region known as the supplementary motor area, which appears to function as a trigger. A fraction of a second before we perform any voluntary act, the 50 million or so neurons in the SMA begin to fire. If you decide to put down this book and brew a cup of coffee, your SMA will start humming. Indeed, it will go into action even if you decide against the coffee and go on reading. If there is any precise area of brain tissue where human volition applies itself, it is here.

But what makes the SMA perk up in the first place? In his answer, Eccles differs from just about everyone else. Somehow the process must begin; an act of conscious volition must occur to start the chain of neurological events. And for Eccles the human will is its own entity, a superior being, independent of neurons and synapses, but empowered to act on them. The will enters the brain through a "liaison area" in the SMA, he suggests, recalling René Descartes's notion of a liaison area in the pineal gland where flesh and spirit interact *(pages 53, 55)*. The will plays upon the SMA's neurons in much the same way that Rudolf Serkin brings forth a Mozart sonata from the keys of a concert piano, Eccles postulates: Mind moves matter by a kind of cerebral psychokinesis.

Again the lines are drawn. Materialists hold that conscious thought arises naturally from the structure of brain tissue, from the intricate wiring of its myriad neurons, and from their response to physical stimuli. For Eccles, it works the other way. Mind is the boss, and it tells the brain exactly what to do.

Although his is a minority view, Eccles has found an influential ally in Sir Karl Popper, a leading philosopher of science. As Popper describes it, mind and brain exist within two separate realities. The brain and all other natural objects belong to world one. The self-conscious mind inhabits the abstract horizons of world two. Beyond both of these lies yet another reality, world three, which embraces the full abundance of the mind's achievements, from the geometry of the pyramids and the sculptures of Michelangelo to skin-cream ads on TV—in short, civilization itself. All three worlds are distinct from each other, yet they continuously interact.

Eccles goes even further. To him, the mind is a God-given entity, incorporeal and unchanging—a direct manifestation, in fact, of the human soul. "Each self is a divine creation," he asserts. His assurance leads well beyond science, of course, and into the wide-open reaches of religious faith. Here it echoes against the age-old wisdom of various sacred texts. "The Supreme Person, of the size of the thumb, dwells forever in the heart of all human beings," reads a passage from the Hindu Upanishads. (Although the Hindu sage may have placed the SMA in the wrong internal organ, he managed to hit upon its correct size.) The New Testament is briefer, if less specific: "The kingdom of heaven is within."

Like the religious visionaries before him, Eccles ponders lofty themes. "I cannot believe," he argues, "that the

Australian neurophysiologist Sir John Carew Eccles, a Nobel laureate, thinks consciousness involves an immaterial mind distinct from the physical brain.

wonderful gift of a conscious existence has no further future, no possibility of another existence under some other unimaginable conditions." Yet Eccles is modest in his faith, and, a good scientist even in his metaphysics, he eschews dogma and keeps clear all avenues for revision and change. "I don't want to claim that I have some extraordinary revelation telling me the answer," Eccles says. "I keep everything open. I keep so many doors open because I am, as it were, a lost soul trying to find my way in the unknown."

Most scientists regard Eccles's conjecture about a disembodied hand manipulating some mental master switch as falling well outside the province of science. The maestro in the brain, some people believe, harks back to the dualism of René Descartes *(pages 50-56)* and is subject to all the same criticisms. It is simply philosopher Gilbert Ryle's "Ghost in the Machine" *(pages 68-69)* dressed up in evening clothes. (Eccles himself admits as much; he is a dualist and proud of it.) And just how does the maestro exert his mysterious influence? No precise mechanism has ever been identified, unless it is a form of psychokinesis pouring in through the supplementary motor area. Besides, many modern theorists find other ways to explain consciousness, using the data at hand.

One is Daniel C. Dennett, professor of science and philosophy at Tufts University. Dennett begins his case by posing an intriguing "thought experiment." Imagine that your brain has been removed from your skull and is being kept alive in a glass jar. A radio network links it to the rest of your body in a system that receives impulses from your senses and broadcasts messages to your muscles. Where is the real you? You can look at the jar and see its contents—clearly outside you. The jar could be shipped to Canada, your brain ticking away inside it, and if the radio link were strong enough, its neurons would still register the sense impressions of your body. Are you at home, or have you moved to Montreal?

The question is unanswerable, says Dennett, because the essential you comprises both your brain and your body acting together. It includes your point of view as experienced through sight and other senses, plus the store of habits, memories, and emotions that have accumulated in your brain circuits.

"This sense of 'I' myself is not a mysterious pearl of mind-stuff, nor is it a little hunk of brain tissue," Dennett maintains. "It's an abstraction. Some abstract objects can be located in space and time—the equator for instance, or the center of gravity of a table lamp. But an abstraction like 'myself' is more difficult to locate because it is the sum of all the activities of my body. 'Myself' is created by my body and brain acting together."

Dennett's profile of the conscious mind comes remarkably close to Sperry's view of consciousness as an abstraction that emerges from the harmonious workings of highly organized gray matter. This thesis is called functionalism, and it is very much in vogue in scientific circles.

No one has done more to promote the functionalist gospel than American physicist and computer scientist Douglas Hofstadter. An occasional collaborator of Dennett's, Hofstadter in 1979 published a groundbreaking volume called *Gödel, Escher, Bach,* which tied together such exciting and diverse topics as baroque music, fabric design, atomic physics, computer science, and human understanding. His point, in essence, is that most things in both art and

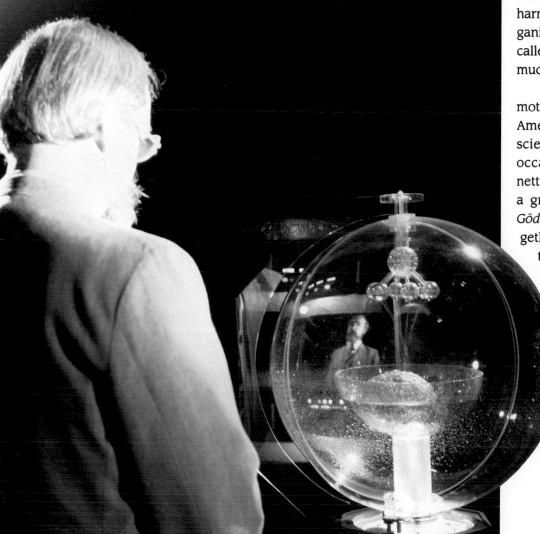

Philosopher Daniel C. Dennett, shown here gazing at a model of a brain, subscribes to the materialist theory that the mind does not exist apart from the brain. He holds that the brain functions in tandem with the body as a single entity.

The Patterns of Visions

In the counterculture of the 1960s, there were many who claimed that hallucinogenic drugs awakened them to soul-enhancing visions—allowing them to see God, perhaps, or to apprehend the meaning of eternity. Experts on hallucination might argue, however, that the visions had less to do with eternity than with electrochemistry: What the visionaries were really seeing were images of their own cerebral landscape.

Ronald K. Siegel is a connoisseur of hallucinations. An experimental psychologist and psychopharmacologist affiliated with the Neuropsychiatric Institute at the University of California at Los Angeles, Siegel has devoted a great deal of his professional life to studying the imaginary sensory experiences connected with psychedelic drugs, epileptic seizures, migraine and cluster headaches, high fevers, and other stimuli that excite the brain into an hallucinatory state. From his extensive studies, Siegel has concluded that because all normal human brains operate in much the same way, they also hallucinate in much the same way. In other words, hallucinations reveal something about the fundamental structure of the human mind, about the patterns that are built into the electrochemical wiring common to all human brains.

The specific images of hallucinations can vary widely from person to person, Siegel has found, depending on each individual's store of memories and personal fantasies; some hallucinations may be glorious visions that evoke religious ecstasy, while others are nightmarish. Moreover, culture helps determine hallucinatory content: Whether we see animals or automobiles, for instance, depends on our everyday environment. Despite differences in imagery, however, Siegel finds that "all hallucinations have the same basic structure." They exhibit a remarkable similarity of form. They progress along similar lines, and there is a great deal of sameness in the ways that their varied elements combine into a total experience.

Furthermore, the scientist has discovered, there are a few simple geometric patterns that occur repeatedly in the early stages of hallucination. Some of the most common are webs, lattices, spiral tunnels, and shapes with the flowerlike symmetry of mandalas. Other researchers exploring this same territory have also found a remarkable uniformity in the patterns "seen" by hallucinating subjects under a wide variety of circumstances.

Some examples of hallucinatory patterns are shown below and opposite.

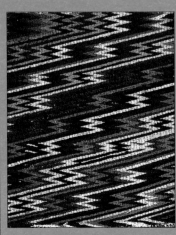   

In an experiment run by psychologist Ronald K. Siegel in Mexico, Huichol Indian weavers were asked to loom images remembered from recent hallucinations induced by peyote and mescaline, drugs commonly used by the Huichol. The patterns resemble designs produced by drug-influenced artisans in many other cultures. Moreover, they have a great deal in common with visions described by religious mystics, epileptics, and others reporting visual hallucinations. Scientists call these recurring patterns hallucinatory constants and believe them to be clues to the brain's storage system for visual data.

An illumination from a twelfth-century manuscript illustrates a vision of Saint Hildegard of Bingen and shows the geometric patterns common to hallucinations. The German nun dictated to a scribe descriptions of what she deemed to be mystic revelations. Modern medicine has diagnosed them instead as hallucinations signaling the onset of migraines. In the picture, a circle representing God surmounts six smaller circles that stand for the days of creation. Adam appears twice in the illustration, once in the Garden of Eden and once after the Fall, with Jesus emerging from the sunrise to save him from his sin.

nature are made up of many small units arranged into over-all patterns. What counts, he says, are not the individual piano notes or the specific brush strokes or the precise detonations of particular nerve cells, but the composite design that links them together. An analogy might be a newspaper photograph that in closeup dissolves into clouds of meaningless dots but that takes on significance when seen from the proper distance.

Or consider the hum and bustle in a colony of ants—one of Hofstadter's favorite images. Each inhabitant plays a well-defined role in the colony's social structure; every ant knows its duty and performs it. At the same time, each individual ant's awareness is extremely limited, and seen in isolation, its actions appear to be random and erratic. But when it functions together with its fellow ants, a grand design emerges. The colony behaves like a single giant organism. It feeds and houses itself, defends itself from danger, propagates itself, and generally exhibits a high degree of seemingly intelligent purpose.

So it is with the human brain—or so the functionalists maintain. The scurrying ants can be likened to our billions of individual neurons, each firing away on signal. Our emergent thoughts are akin to the colony's sophisticated social network and its community of purpose.

nother metaphor borrows from computer science. On one level, a desktop IBM or Macintosh does its computing by means of silicon chips that contain thousands of tiny electronic switches. They are the key components of the computer's mechanical hardware, and their operation is analogous to the current-regulating function of the brain's synaptic connectors. A computer must be programmed before it can work, however, so it is given a set of instructions, its software. The software is, at root, simply a set of electric on-or-off signals—an abstraction—like the mind itself. Smash any individual IBM, and the same program can be run in almost any other IBM. Without its program, a computer is an inert piece of machinery. With it, the computer can add and subtract, move paragraphs, draw pictures, play chess, and perform complex calculations.

To a functionalist, the program is a pattern of activity, and it is linked to the computer's hardware through the exchange of information. Although one is abstract and the other mechanical, no conflict exists between them. No mind over matter, no ghost in the microchips. Instead, there is a system of communication. A similar process may give rise to human awareness, the functionalists maintain. As Douglas Hofstadter puts it, "My belief is that the explanations of 'emergent' phenomena in our brains—for instance, ideas, hopes, images, analogies, and finally consciousness and free will—are based on . . . an interaction between levels in which the top level reaches back down to the bottom level and influences it."

Given the seeming parallels between brains and computers, some people wonder whether computers will one day start thinking on their own. Perhaps science will devise chips of such extraordinary complexity and sophistication that they will spontaneously generate their own electronic feelings and aspirations, their own variety of self-awareness. But if a computer can ever be endowed with powers resembling human intelligence, will it have what amounts to consciousness, intentionality, subjectivity? Will it possess a soul?

Nothing in functionalist dogma declares that computers must be soulless. Since the conscious mind arises from a pattern of activity—from structure, not substance—it hardly matters whether the components in the structure are nerve cells, silicon chips, or some other type of unimagined unit belonging to alien creatures from outer space. According to Jerry Fodor, a professor of philosophy and psychology at Massachusetts Institute of Technology and a leading spokesman of functionalism, "The software description of the mind does not logically require neurons. . . . Functionalism recognizes the possibility that systems as diverse as human beings, calculating machines, and disembodied spirits could all have mental states."

Science has other ways of looking at the mind, some even broader in their implications. If thoughts are a process in the brain and are not always confined to particular sections of gray matter, it seems only sensible to consider their relationship to the brain as a whole. The whole may add up to far more than the sum of its parts.

A surprising discovery by British neurologist John Lorber offers an example of this proposition. Lorber specializes in the treatment of hydrocephalus, or water on the brain, in which large quantities of fluid build up in the cerebral cavities. The condition usually begins in early childhood, and it marks its victims by giving them abnormally large heads. It also destroys brain cells, which are crowded out by the invading fluid.

hen he diagnoses a patient, Lorber calls for a CAT scan, an x-ray-like procedure that reveals the brain's interior structure. One test subject, chosen because his cranium was slightly larger than normal, was a university student working toward a high honors degree in mathematics. Aside from his large hat size and an above-average IQ of 126, he seemed normal. But the CAT scan revealed that most of his brain was missing. "Instead of the normal 4.5-centimeter thickness of brain tissue between the ventricles and the cortical surface," Lorber reported, "there was just a thin layer of mantle. His cranium was mainly filled with cerebrospinal fluid."

How could this be? Lacking most of his cortex, the supposed site of higher intelligence, the student should have been a walking vegetable. He was far from it, however, and systematic research on other hydrocephalics told a similar story. Even with subjects whose skulls were 95 percent awash in fluid, only a few were retarded or disabled. Half had IQs greater than 100. Relating his findings at a pediatrics conference in 1980, Lorber posed the question, half jokingly: "Is your brain really necessary?"

It is, of course, but clearly not all of it is. Much of the brain's capacity, particularly in the cortex, may be redundant—extra storage space that simply goes unused, gathering brain dust. Or, as the functionalists suggest, the number of brain cells may be less important than the efficiency of the circuitry between those few that remain.

A more tantalizing interpretation is also more sweepingly holistic. It maintains that any single part of the cortex, if properly wired, will perform the same work as the cortex as a whole. This, at any rate, is the conclusion espoused by Karl Pribram as he darts between the computer screens, testing devices, and photo-imaging apparatus in his office at Stanford University's psychology lab. Pribram has devoted his career to the phenomenon of memory. For years he poked into the skulls of chimpanzees, plugging in electrodes and measuring the current in hopes of discovering a physiological code that controls memory storage and retrieval. Eventually, he decided that there is no specific code—or rather, that the code is nowhere and everywhere at the same time. According to Pribram, the mind works like a hologram.

A hologram is a three-dimensional photograph created by laser lights. A laser is a type of illumination composed of a single wavelength. To make a hologram, the photographer splits a laser beam in half. One half is aimed directly at a piece of holographic film. The other half is bounced off the object to be photographed and ricocheted onto the film. When the two halves meet on the film, they form a nebulous, swirling pattern. But later, after the film is developed, the magic occurs. When another laser, called a reconstruction beam, passes through the film, the object's three-dimensional image will appear in space, insubstantial as a desert mirage but real nonetheless. Furthermore, any portion of the film will serve to re-create the entire image. The photographer can focus his reconstruction laser through the full strip of celluloid or through a mere fragment and the effect will be the same. All the pertinent information has been captured by every square micromillimeter of film.

No laser beams streak through our gray cells, to be sure, but the principle may be the same. "I'm simply saying

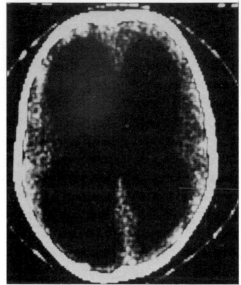

that our brains use a holographic-like code," Pribram explains. "The brain performs certain operations, which can be described by the mathematics of holography, to code, decode, and record sensory imput."

The hologram hypothesis would answer some awkward questions about memory and consciousness—why laboratory rats with massive brain damage can still remember their path through mazes, for example, and why a hydrocephalic with not much brain at all can win high honors in math. Because of the hologram's immense storage capacity, the analogy explains how all we know and imagine—our memories of childhood, our regrets and aspirations, our visions of the universe—can be wedged into three pounds of flesh about the size of a grapefruit. It also casts light on the old controversy between the materialists and the dualists over the relationship between the brain and the mind, or soul. And it beacons ahead to more promising horizons. "The mind isn't located in a place," Pribram suggests. "What we have is holographic-like machinery that turns out images, which we perceive as existing somewhere outside the machine that produces them. . . . Dualism's okay for the Newtonian domain. But it doesn't apply to the holographic, enfolded order. There is no space and time, no causality, no matter and no mind. Everything is enfolded. There are no boundaries."

An unfolded consciousness, unbounded and infinite—the search for the soul sweeps out toward the furthest reaches of time and space to the windy amplitudes of cosmic geography and astrophysics, where such concepts prevail. At the same time, it focuses in on the tiniest units of

CAT scan images show the almost total absence of brain (top) in a young man of high intelligence (page 129), compared with a normal brain (bottom).

matter and energy, to the looking-glass algebra of quantum mechanics. It is at these extremes of nature that the standard laws of cause and effect break down: Space curves, light waves become particles, and the flow of time expands and contracts like a rubber band. There is room enough in these eerie dimensions, certain theorists believe, for a spectral intelligence that travels across all barriers, a free-floating consciousness that suffuses the entire universe. A collective mind, perhaps—a cosmic soul.

The barriers began to fall at the beginning of this century with a whirlwind of discoveries in the physical sciences. Albert Einstein helped lead the way with his theory of relativity. The thought that time is elastic, that there is an equivalence between energy and mass, and that what you see as true depends on where you happen to be standing set classical physics on its head. Such notions, almost impossible to visualize, could only be expressed in the abstract language of mathematics. The basic cosmic reality came to be seen not so much as energy, matter, time, and space, but as the complex equations that describe them—equations that are themselves a construct of human intelligence. Announced the great astronomer Sir Arthur Eddington, whose observations during a 1919 solar eclipse helped prove Einstein correct about relativity: "The stuff of the world is mind stuff."

Some physicists have suggested that the universe itself can be seen as a giant hologram. According to David Bohm of the University of London, each cluster of stars and every spinning atom somehow bears within it the total cosmos. We live enmeshed in a seamless, multidimensional fabric of being and nonbeing, Bohm claims, in which mind and matter appear as ripples on a vast ocean of pulsating energy. All creation is mysteriously connected "in a state of unending flux of enfoldment and unfoldment," he says, "with laws much of which are only vaguely understood." The concept calls to mind ancient precepts of the Tao, the Chinese philosophy of a universe made up of contending, interdependent opposites, forever in flux, or the equally old Hindu notions of the cosmos as an unending and all-encompassing cycle of creation, destruction, and rebirth.

Bohm is a student of the Indian philosopher Krishnamurti, a fact that helps to explain the scientist's out-

spokenly mystical turn of mind. He is also a leading authority on quantum mechanics, one who has gained respect for his research into the exotic behavior of subatomic particles. And the behavior of these tiny entities that physicists call quanta—creation's building blocks—seems mystical indeed.

Take the structure of an ordinary light beam, which to quantum theory consists of a stream of energy-carrying particles called photons. The photons spurt out from their source like so many machine-gun bullets. Should they strike a light-sensitive target, such as the electric eye in a supermarket doorway, they knock out electrons and generate a current. But a light beam is also a wave sequence, which undulates through space according to the same mathematical laws that govern the movement of waves across water. The light assumes either guise, particles or waves, depending on the instruments used to measure it. By way of instrumentation, the observer decides, the light beam complies. In a sense, the watcher's very act of watching has determined physical reality.

A similar paradox was discovered by the German physicist Werner Heisenberg, who found he could learn either the position of a particle or else its momentum, but not both precisely at once. The standard method of observation, tracking a particle's path through a cloud chamber, distorted the results in one property or the other. Eventu-

Neurophysiologist Karl Pribram points to a strip of holographic film, which encodes images in such a way that any fragment of the film can reproduce the entire picture. Pribram says the mind encodes content much the same way: The whole is contained in every part. "Mind isn't located in a place," the scientist declares.

Souls in Suspension

While some modern scientists search for a soul that goes on to another life, others concentrate on preserving and extending the one life humans can grasp with empirical certainty—the one they are living. The scientific quest for longer life can be as mundane as nutrition and exercise studies, as exotic as research seeking to unravel the genetic causes of physical aging, or as bizarrely futuristic as cryonics, the still-unproven practice of freezing people at death in hopes of thawing them out later when medical science has progressed sufficiently to restore their preserved bodies to full health and vigor. Cryonicists, like more orthodox scientists engaged in research to prolong life, do not address the question of the soul; they are not concerned with the definition of life as some subtle spiritual essence distinct from the physical self, only with the biological processes that differentiate a living organism from a dead one.

In the minds of many medical researchers, cryonics is a disreputable cousin to the legitimate practice of cryobiology, the use of extreme cold to preserve human tissues for later use. Cryobiology has had some notable medical triumphs: Blood has been successfully transfused after being frozen for as long as sixteen years; and "test tube babies" have been born from frozen embryos, as well as from eggs and sperm cells that were held in cold storage before being thawed out for fertilization. Surgeons are exploring new frontiers in cryobiology as they work with frozen and thawed tissues in transplanting corneas, heart valves, and kidneys. But efforts to freeze and restore larger organs have not met with long-term success because too many of their cells suffer damage from freezing. Thus most scientists remain skeptical—not to say derisive—about the prospects for cryonic preservation of an entire body.

"Large pieces of tissue are not able to be frozen," states Dr. Stanley Leibo, a cryobiologist on the faculty of the Baylor University College of Medicine. Describing cryonics as "fraudulent," Leibo suggests that even if it were possible to preserve and then revive a whole body, cryonicists play "a bit of logical magic" in assuming the resurrected body could be healed of whatever afflicted it prior to freezing. As Leibo points out, there is no guarantee science will ever conquer all diseases.

Nevertheless, believers in cryonics point to experiments with dogs and hamsters. Some of these living mammals have been cooled to just a few degrees above freezing, drained of their blood, transfused with chemical solutions that combat low-temperature cell damage, and finally brought back to warm-blooded life. Even though these animals were merely cooled—not frozen—cryonics enthusiasts maintain that the mammal experiments hold immense promise. The tests indicate, proponents say, that living bodies of terminally ill humans will someday be able to undergo similar treatment and awaken to new life after a long hiatus in a tank full of liquid nitrogen.

For the moment, however, the terminally ill are not at issue. Companies that offer cryonic storage deal only with corpses—never with clients who are still alive. All the cryonic customers currently on ice in hopes of cheating death are people who were frozen right after dying.

Preparation of a corpse for long-term

Miles, a beagle named for the cryonically preserved character played by actor Woody Allen in the 1973 movie Sleeper, came to national attention in 1987 when experimenters replaced his blood with a glycerol solution. The canine, while alive, was cooled to a few degrees above freezing, then was revived after spending fifteen minutes in this state of "suspended animation."

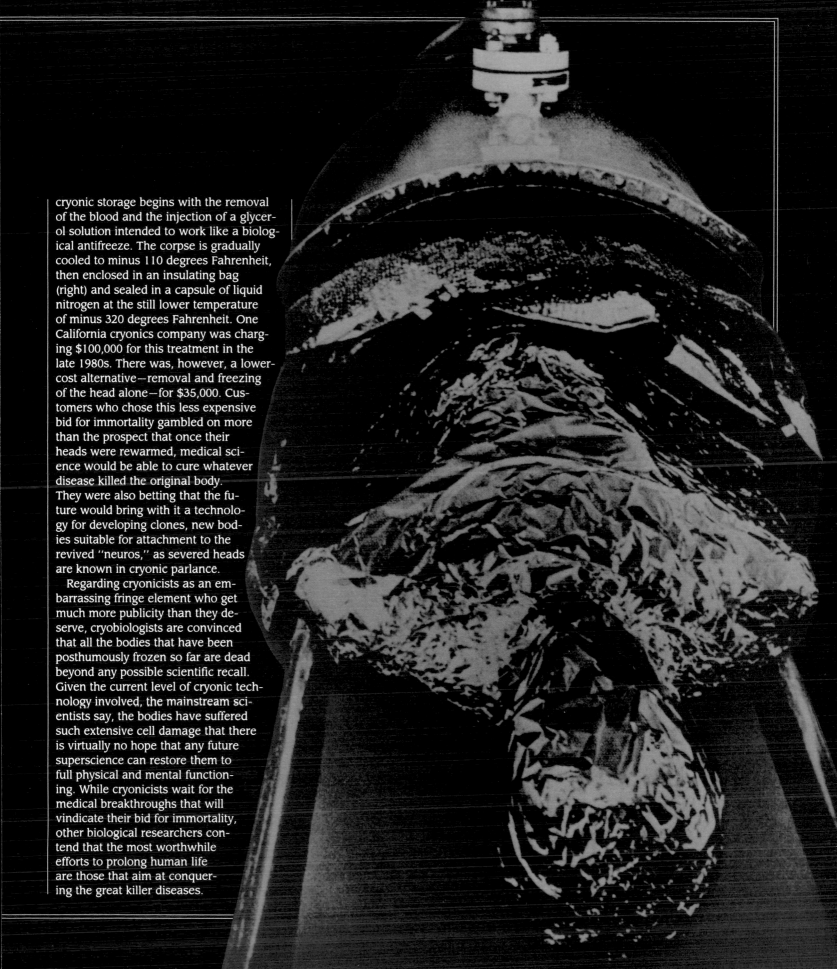

cryonic storage begins with the removal
of the blood and the injection of a glycerol solution intended to work like a biological antifreeze. The corpse is gradually
cooled to minus 110 degrees Fahrenheit,
then enclosed in an insulating bag
(right) and sealed in a capsule of liquid
nitrogen at the still lower temperature
of minus 320 degrees Fahrenheit. One
California cryonics company was charg-
ing $100,000 for this treatment in the
late 1980s. There was, however, a lower-
cost alternative—removal and freezing
of the head alone—for $35,000. Cus-
tomers who chose this less expensive
bid for immortality gambled on more
than the prospect that once their
heads were rewarmed, medical science would be able to cure whatever
disease killed the original body.
They were also betting that the future would bring with it a technology for developing clones, new bodies suitable for attachment to the
revived "neuros," as severed heads
are known in cryonic parlance.

Regarding cryonicists as an em-
barrassing fringe element who get
much more publicity than they de-
serve, cryobiologists are convinced
that all the bodies that have been
posthumously frozen so far are dead
beyond any possible scientific recall.
Given the current level of cryonic technology involved, the mainstream scientists say, the bodies have suffered
such extensive cell damage that there
is virtually no hope that any future
superscience can restore them to
full physical and mental functioning. While cryonicists wait for the
medical breakthroughs that will
vindicate their bid for immortality,
other biological researchers contend that the most worthwhile
efforts to prolong human life
are those that aim at conquer-
ing the great killer diseases.

ally, Heisenberg concluded that the basic properties of any one particle can never be established with absolute precision. The more exact the measurement of one property, the less exact the measurement of the other. This finding of quantum mechanics, now almost universally accepted, is known as the uncertainty principle—a direct assault on the principle of causality in physics.

So fuzzy is the nature of subatomic relationships, in fact, that some physicists contend the very act of observation is needed to give these fragments their place in the scheme of things. Unless you hunt for a photon or an electron, it remains, for the observer's purposes, a ghost. Look for the photon's location and it becomes a photon with an address. Look for its motion and it becomes a photon with speed. It cannot be seen to be both at once, due to the effects of the measuring device on subatomic objects.

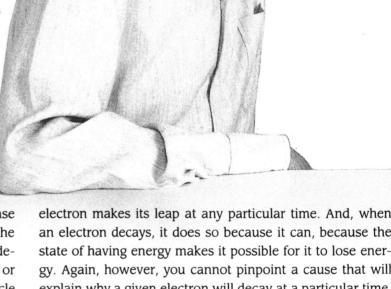

Quantum theory leads down still weirder corridors. The picture on an ordinary television screen is a case in point. It is formed by a beam of electrons hitting the screen's fluorescent coating. But there is no sure way of determining where any particular electron will show up or what fragment of the picture it will produce. The particle leaves an electrode at the back of the TV tube, and it pops up somewhere on the screen's face, but by quantum dictates it has made no predictable passage between the two.

Similarly quirky effects mark the behavior of electrons within the energy levels—sometimes likened to shells—that encompass each atomic nucleus. If an electron absorbs packets of energy, it will become "excited," as quantum theory has it, jumping to a higher energy level in a "quantum leap." If it emits energy, it will "decay," as physicists term the phenomenon, falling to a lower energy level. But what causes it to change? In answering, physicists make some fine distinctions. For instance, when an electron becomes excited by absorbing energy, the energy source is, in one sense, the cause of the excitation. But it is not the whole cause; rather, it is what allows the possibility for the excitation. It does not explain why any particular

electron makes its leap at any particular time. And, when an electron decays, it does so because it can, because the state of having energy makes it possible for it to lose energy. Again, however, you cannot pinpoint a cause that will explain why a given electron will decay at a particular time.

The shadowy nature of causality in all this has certain consequences. It is possible to make statistical predictions about electrons' behavior—when they are apt to gain or lose energy—just as it is possible to calculate the odds of turning up double sixes in a certain number of dice tosses. You can describe what is probable but not what is certain. You cannot predict with absolute confidence what any particular electron will do at any given time. The electron leaps or decays arbitrarily, with no discernable event—no hand on the causal master switch—to prompt its energy gain or energy loss. This is a fact that even such a mind as Einstein's found difficult to accept, given his belief that knowing all there was to know about a system guaranteed that you could confidently predict all its workings. "God does not play dice with the universe," the patriarch of relativity famously harrumphed.

"Everything interpenetrates everything," says American physicist David Bohm (near left), pictured here at a 1985 meeting with Indian mystic Jiddu Krishnamurti. Bohm, whose study of subatomic particles has been strongly influenced by Eastern mysticism, contends that human consciousness should be regarded as part of a unity that includes the entire universe.

Einstein was equally disturbed by another peculiarity of the quantum world. Suppose an atom decays, releasing two particles that go spinning off in opposite directions. Because of a basic natural law, if one particle spins clockwise its companion will have to spin counterclockwise. But according to quantum theory, the direction of spin can only be established by observation. Indeed, it suggests that both particles are programmed with the built-in potential to spin both ways. So off the particles fly, racing perhaps several light-years apart, each carrying two possibilities. Then if someone looks at the left-hand particle, the very act of observation will show its spin potential to "collapse" into the reality of a clockwise or counterclockwise motion. At the very same instant, billions of miles away, the other particle takes up the opposite spin.

This bizarre state of affairs has been proved by experiment. Yet every explanation leads into the realm of the seemingly impossible. At the moment of observation, either time runs backward, to re-create the original tick of the particles' release, or else the particles remain in communication over the vast distances of space and time that separate them, thereby defying the precept that there is nothing that moves faster than the speed of light. Or else they are part of the same cosmic totality, units in a single holographic continuum that embraces not only them, but the span of their separation and the instrumentation of the scientist who has observed them.

The thought that human consciousness can determine events in the physical world preoccupies a group of senior scientists with the Princeton Engineering Anomalies Research project at Princeton University. A few years ago Robert G. Jahn, Princeton's dean of engineering, was engaged in propulsion research for America's space program. He became aware of a suspicious pattern of technical glitches in equipment that performed microelectronic information processing, guidance, and control, and he began to think some of the problems might lie with the moods and thoughts of the equipment's human operators. So, in collaboration with psychologist Brenda J. Dunne, he devised a series of experiments to test the idea.

PEAR addressed itself to exploring the effect of human consciousness on the workings of inanimate machinery. One of the machines that Jahn and Dunne chose for the work was a computerized device that spews out binary numbers, plus ones and minus ones, in random sequence—a kind of electronic coin flipper. A human operator tries to influence the machine's output through conscious intent, willing it to generate more pluses than minuses or vice versa. The results are then compared with the fifty-fifty distribution attributable to chance.

So far, the PEAR laboratory has run more than one million trials and found that a number of operators do indeed seem able to influence the results. Some can produce more pluses, some more minuses, and some can do both. Some even produce effects consistently opposite to their intentions. The deviations in the tests are slight, only about

Experiments reported by Princeton University researchers Robert G. Jahn and Brenda J. Dunne in their book Margins of Reality suggest that human consciousness can affect inanimate matter.

one coin toss per thousand. But, according to the researchers, they are statistically significant.

Another type of experiment in the PEAR lab tests human abilities in extrasensory perception. An "agent" pays a visit to a randomly chosen spot, and a "percipient" tries to visualize the agent's whereabouts. Again, the results are startling. An agent heads for the railroad station at Glencoe, Illinois, and the percipient in Chicago describes a public setting of wall posters, littered wooden floors—and arriving trains. Another percipient summons up an image of a heavy wooden door, rounded at the top, which he mentally opens. Inside all is dark and quiet, with rows of high-backed wooden benches. "My feeling at this moment is that it's a church," he says. One hour and fifteen minutes later, the agent enters a randomly selected target, the Rockefeller Chapel at the University of Chicago.

Not all percipients' visions are as precise as this one, and some misfire completely. But their accuracy beats out chance by some 15 percent, say Jahn and Dunne. Distance is no impediment, it seems. A viewer in New York City described a scene at Loch Ness through the eyes of an agent on the spot and sketched the ruins of a Scottish castle the agent was gazing at. Another in Wisconsin located an agent on the Danube River in Czechoslovakia.

Nor is time necessarily a limiting factor, according to the PEAR team. Percipients can sometimes re-create sites after the agents have left them or before they have arrived. In many cases, Jahn and Dunne report, talented viewers have described sites even before the research team has had a chance to select them. The researchers can only conclude that in some as yet inexplicable way, consciousness helps determine reality.

It is the mission of science to explain, however, so Jahn and Dunne are attempting to come up with a theory. In their book, entitled *Margins of Reality,* the experimenters suggest that consciousness follows much the same laws as quantum mechanics. For certain purposes, consciousness may be regarded as a well-defined particle, sharply localized in space and time, interacting with its environment much like a gas molecule does. But on other occasions, consciousness may act like waves of energy, rippling out across space and time and establishing subtle resonances with other consciousnesses and with its material environment. Jahn and Dunne believe that it is this latter, wavelike character that accounts for some of the anomalies turned up by their experiments. Just as waves in a bathtub take their shape in part from the dimensions of the tub, our thoughts and experiences are shaped by the nature of our environment. But if the tub overflows or shatters, the waves become freely propagating, like thoughts that range beyond their normal spatial and temporal limits.

In support of their views, Jahn and Dunne like to quote German quantum physicist Wolfgang Pauli, who was also a believer in parapsychological effects: "The microphysical world of the atom exhibits certain features whose affinities with the psyche have impressed themselves even on the physicists." And so the two Princeton investigators join the growing number of scientists and philosophers who acknowledge the possibility of a free-flowing, noncausal interchange between matter and the human spirit. The laws

Half a Mystic

"It's hard to understand where thoughts and creativity come from using traditional scientific approaches," says Welsh scientist Brian Josephson. His own exceptional thoughts and creativity won him the 1973 Nobel prize in physics for work he had done over a decade earlier as a twenty-two-year-old graduate student at England's Cambridge University, where he is now a professor. One of the youngest Nobelists in the prize's history, he shared it with two colleagues. Their groundbreaking research was in the field of superconductivity, the phenomenon of zero resistance to electricity of some metals below a critical temperature.

Since becoming a Nobel laureate, Josephson has come to be known as one of the scientific community's most distinguished believers that a dimension of reality lies beyond the reach of Western science. He first pursued an understanding of this dimension through Transcendental Meditation and more recently took up raja-yoga, an ancient Eastern system that includes meditation and also entails other stringent mental and physical disciplines. Through these practices, Josephson became convinced of the existence of a soul that survives physical death. "One is not the same as one's body," says Josephson, who describes the soul as a nonphysical "organizing center" of the self.

Describing himself as "half a mystic," Josephson once told an interviewer, "As a scientist, I am interested in seeking fundamentally new insights into the nature of reality." Like Sir John Eccles *(pages 123-124),* David Bohm *(pages 130-131, 135),* and other scientists whose studies incorporate spiritual methods for exploring the nature of reality, Josephson has found that his mystical outlook attracts considerable skepticism even from colleagues who admire his work in traditional physics.

"The meditation-yoga goes beyond a sensory level, to a different 'thinking,' " Josephson counters. "People who say no to a central organizing center have an approach that is too simple. There is an appreciating level of experience different from experiencing your body." Noting a "generalized development" in his own sense of self, the scientist says he is "more aware of the outside world and my relationships to people than I was earlier." He persists in believing that physical science alone will never reveal a complete picture of reality and that an intelligent world view has to incorporate elements of both rational thought and mystical insight.

Brian Josephson contends that out-of-body experiences are among the paranormal phenomena arguing for the existence of a human soul that is separable from the body.

The Search for Ensoulment

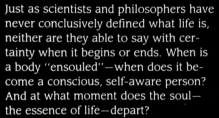

Just as scientists and philosophers have never conclusively defined what life is, neither are they able to say with certainty when it begins or ends. When is a body "ensouled"—when does it become a conscious, self-aware person? And at what moment does the soul—the essence of life—depart?

Some medical and religious thinkers through the ages have maintained that quickening, the onset of fetal movement in the womb, indicates the start of life. But modern medical science has learned to measure a subtler kind of quickening—the electrical activity of the fetal brain. Rudimentary brain activity can be detected when an embryo is eight weeks old. Electrical activity in the cerebrum, the area that is the seat of consciousness, begins during the fetus's sixth month. Some doctors see this milestone as the beginning of self-awareness. A fetus such as the one seen here, sixteen weeks old and just over six inches long, would show some electrical activity in its developing nervous system, but no higher brain activity. The question of whether it is a "living person" is still open to debate.

The identification of life with brain activity is a fairly new medical concept, but one with critical relevance for determining death as well. For generations, doctors looked for signs of breathing and heartbeat to tell whether a patient was still alive. Today "brain death," the cessation of electrical signals in the brain, is widely seen as the sign of life's end. But even this is subject to revision. Some doctors propose refining the term to include the "cognitive death" of irreversible coma, in which intellect, memory, speech, and self-awareness are gone, although the brain is still capable of reflex functions—breathing, sleeping, and digestion. So when does the moment of death arrive? With cardiovascular death, with the loss of all brain function, or with the loss of self-awareness? "There is no moment of death," says Dr. Julius Korein, professor of neurology at New York University School of Medicine and chairman of Bellevue Hospital's ethics committee. "Look at cardiovascular death. The heart stops. The doctor listens to the chest. Was that the moment of death? With modern equipment, you can detect signs of electrical activity in the heart forty minutes after it has stopped beating. The moment of death is a fiction."

Whatever the answers as to when life begins and ends, the questions are no longer just abstract. They are crucial to ongoing ethical debates over matters such as abortion and human organ transplant—issues important to law, medicine, and humanity in general.

of interaction remain murky, and proof is elusive. But even Einstein saw a connection. "Body and soul," he wrote, "are not two separate things, but only two ways of perceiving the same thing."

Large questions remain, of course, including the ultimate one: Does the soul survive the extinction of the body? Given that the stuff of the universe is indestructible and, like matter into energy, can only be transformed from one form of experience into another, does it not follow that if the soul is a reality, in whatever form, it must live on, perhaps in some altered state? Sir John Eccles has declared that it does. Physicist David Bohm also implies as much, asserting the timeless durability of the holographic continuum. Jahn and Dunne, too, see free-moving waves of consciousness, released from their mortal environment, rippling on indefinitely.

But the puzzle lingers. To be sure, recent developments in theoretical physics have shown the cosmos to be a dynamic process that has never been fully defined or known, one in which the whole is exemplified only in its parts, which are themselves elusive. The same description might also apply to human consciousness—a fact that has led some scientists to theorize that the cosmos is itself conscious, a continuity of the inorganic, organic, and mental. But does such theory suffice to establish the primacy of consciousness in the universe? Can science, faith's old enemy, resurrect that faith and reestablish a certainty of God and a soul? No, its critics say   at least not yet, and perhaps never. Scientists enter philosophy and theology as amateurs, after all, permitting latitude in reasoning that they would never tolerate in their own disciplines. Some new cosmology may be in the making, but it is far too soon to perceive its lineaments or describe its final reality.

Nor have the parapsychologists found the soul. All attempt at communication between the living and the departed is ambiguous at best, and even the most vivid reports from those who claim to have gone on out-of-body journeys to the threshold of the beyond do not bear the weight of hard, empirical proof. If our souls are swept into the continuum, or translated into whirls of cosmic light, can they still be aware of what is happening to them? As philosophy professor Michael Grosso of Jersey City State College points out, if personality survives in this manner, it ceases to be truly personal. Even Carl Jung, that champion of paranormal flights of fancy, hedged on this issue. "We lack concrete proof that anything of us is preserved for eternity," he admitted. "At most we can say that our psyche continues beyond physical death. Whether what continues is conscious of itself, we do not know."

And here the matter stands. This book has told how some years ago, a grizzled old prospector by the name of James Kidd died leaving a legacy, with instructions that it be used to resolve this issue. In 1975, the American Society for Psychical Research, recipient of the lion's share of Kidd's money, reported to the probate court in Phoenix, Arizona, on what it had discovered.

tarting in 1971, the researchers spent $275,455, most of it on recording the death-bed experiences of people in the United States and India. In both countries, the report said, it seemed that death might turn out to be life's greatest adventure, a joyful and vibrant revelation. Whether Eastern or Western, said the ASPR, the dying subjects described "visions, perceptions, or increased brightness, very intense, fully saturated colors, and elation." On the whole, said the parapsychology experts, death seemed to impart a sense of "incredible freedom, harmony, and wholeness." But as to the human soul—what it is and where it goes—the ASPR could say nothing conclusive. Perhaps James Kidd would have been disappointed. On the other hand, by that time he had made the journey himself. Maybe he knew the answers firsthand.

The ASPR's report was duly chronicled by the *New York Times* in its issue of June 16, 1975, under the headline, "Researchers Aided by Hermit's Will Fail to Find a Soul." The story appeared on the *Times*'s obituary page.

ACKNOWLEDGMENTS

The editors thank these individuals and institutions for their valuable assistance in the preparation of this volume: François Avril, Conservateur, Département des Manuscrits, Bibliothèque Nationale, Paris; Brigitte Baumbusch, Scala, Florence, Italy; Professor Hans Bender, Institut für Grenzgebiete der Psychologie und Psychohygiene, Freiburg, West Germany; Mike Darwin, Alco Life Extension Foundation, Riverside, Calif.; Brenda Dunne, Princeton Engineering Anomalies Research, N.J.; R. A. Gilbert, Bristol, England; Professor Robert Jahn, Princeton University, N.J.; Professor Brian Josephson, Cambridge, England; Michael Lee, The Hutchison Library, London; Dr. Stanley Liebo, Baylor College of Medicine, Houston, Tex.; Professor Andreas Lommel, Munich, West Germany; Professor John Lorber, Gloucestershire, England; Marie Montembault, Documentaliste, Département des Antiquités Grecques et Romaines, Musée du Louvre, Paris; Tim Nicholson, London; Eleanor O'Keeffe, The Society for Psychical Research, London; Louisa Ricciarini, Milan; Professor William G. Roll, West Georgia College, Carrollton; Dr. Ronald K. Siegel, Los Angeles, Calif.; Colin Smythe, Buckinghamshire, England; Dr. Rolf Streichardt, Institut für Grenzgebiete der Psychologie und Psychohygiene, Freiburg, West Germany; Alan Wesencraft, Harry Price Library, London.

PICTURE CREDITS

The sources for the illustrations in this book are shown below. Credits from left to right are separated by semicolons; credits from top to bottom are separated by dashes.

Cover art by Kimmerle Milnazik. 7: Art by Bryan Leister. 8, 9: D. Dietrich/FPG International; AP/Wide World Photos (2). 10: Adam Woolfitt/Susan Griggs Agency, London. 11: Janet and Colin Bord, Corwen, Clwyd, Scotland; From *Mystic Spiral*, by Jill Purse, Thames and Hudson, London, 1974 —Tony Morrison/South American Pictures, Woodbridge, Suffolk. 13: Werner Forman Archive/Eugene Chesrow Trust, London. 14: Bill and Claire Leimbach, Avalon, NSW, Australia. 16, 17: The Metropolitan Museum of Art, Fletcher Fund, 1963 (63.210.11); courtesy The Trustees of the British Museum, London; Charles Lenars/Explorer, Paris. 19: Baschieri Salvadori, from *Man, Myth and Magic*, ed. by Richard Cavendish, Marshall Cavendish Ltd., London, 1983. 20: Scala, Florence, courtesy Biblioteca Nazionale Centrale, Florence. 22, 23: Victor Englebert. 24: Christian Kallen. 25: Michael MacIntyre/The Hutchison Library, London. 27: Courtesy The Trustees of the British Museum, London. 29: Courtesy The Trustees of the British Museum, London; The Museum of Fine Arts, Boston (2). 30, 31: By Sam Abell/© 1984 National Geographic Society. 33: Hans-Jürgen Burkard/Bilderberg, Hamburg. 34: Hiroshi Suga. 35: Bruno Barbey, Magnum. 36, 37: Michael MacIntyre/The Hutchison Library, London; Leonard Lueras/Image Network Indonesia, Bali. 38, 39: Christian Kallen (2). 40, 41: Hans-Jürgen Burkard/Bilderberg, Hamburg. 43: Art by Bryan Leister. 45: R. Spencer Stanhope/The City Art Gallery, Manchester. 47: Scala, Florence, courtesy Museo Archeologico Nazionale, Naples. 48: William Blake, courtesy The Trustees of the British Museum, London. 50: Bibliothèque Nationale, Paris. 51: Scala, Florence, courtesy Il Duomo, Orvieto. 52: Edimedia/Archives Snark, Paris. 53: Courtesy The Trustees of the British Library, London. 54: Harley MS3469 f24, courtesy The Trustees of the British Library, London. 59: Bildarchiv Preussischer Kulturbesitz, West Berlin. 60: Mansell Collection, London. 64-66: Mary Evans Picture Library, London. 67: Werner Forman Archive/Private Collection, London. 69: Studio Basset, courtesy Musée des Beaux Arts, Lyons. 70: Art by Dana Verkouteren. 71: Roger-Viollet, Paris. 72-87: Gustave Doré, from the *Divine Comedy*, by Dante Alighieri, courtesy Library of Congress. 89: Art by Bryan Leister. 90: Arnold Desser, from *Is There Life after Death?* by Robert Kastenbaum, Multimedia Productions (UK), London, 1984. 91: Jean-Loup Charmet, Paris. 93: Al Freni, drawing by Frederic Thompson, courtesy American Society of Psychical Research, New York. 94, 95: from "The Unexplained," vol. 11, issue 122, Orbis Ltd., London, 1983 (3). 96: Mary Evans Picture Library/Society for Psychical Research, London. 98: The Granger Collection, New York. 100, 101: BPCC/Aldus Archive, London. 103: Goetheanum Verlag, Dornach, Switzerland—© Claire Mohr, 1988, Goetheanum Verlag, Dornach, Switzerland. 105: Colin Smythe, Gerrards Cross, Buckinghamshire (2). 106: Courtesy The College of Psychic Studies, London, from *Swan on a Black Sea*, by Geraldine Cummins, ed. by Signe Toksvig, Routledge and Kegan Paul, London, 1965; Mary Evans Picture Library/Society for Psychical Research, London. 109-113: The College of Psychic Studies, London, from *A Goodly Company*, by Ethel Le Rossignol. 115: Art by Bryan Leister. 116: Courtesy WNET/13 and Richard Restak, M.D., from *The Brain*, by Richard Restak, Bantum Books, New York, 1984. 119: The Mansell Collection, London; Archiv für Kunst und Geschichte, West Berlin; Mary Evans Picture Library, London (2). 121: Christopher Springman. 122: Art by Sam Ward. 124: Camera Press, London. 125: Mat Irvine, London. 126: Ronald K. Siegel. 127: Otto Mueller Verlag, Salzburg, from *Scivias*, Hildegard von Bingen. 130: Professor John Lorber, Tewkesbury, Gloucestershire (2). 131: Courtesy Stanford University Photo Department. 132: Custom Medical Stock Photo/© 1989 M. Fisher. 133: Rex Features, London. 134, 135: Photo Mark Edwards, London/© Krishnamurti Foundation Trust. 136: Karen Halverson. 137: Manni Masons Pictures, Cambridge. 138: Photo by Lennart Nilsson from *Behold Man*, by Lennart Nilsson, Little, Brown & Co., Boston, 1973

BIBLIOGRAPHY

Adler, Mortimer F.:
The Angels and Us. New York: Macmillan, 1982.
The Difference of Man and the Difference It Makes. New York: Holt, Rinehart and Winston, 1967.
Alighieri, Dante, *The Divine Comedy.* Transl. by Lawrence Grant White. New York: Pantheon Books, 1948.
Allen, Gay Wilson, *William James.* New York, Viking Press, 1967.
Almeder, Robert, *Beyond Death.* Springfield, Ill.: Charles C. Thomas, 1987.
Alston, William P., and Richard B. Brandt, eds., *The Problems of Philosophy.* Boston: Allyn and Bacon, 1978.
Alvarado, Carlos S., "Phenomenological Aspects of Out-of-Body Experiences: A Report of Three Studies." *Journal of the American Society for Psychical Research,* July 1984.
Anderson, Roger I., "Reincarnation: A New Horizon in Science, Religion, and Society, by Sylvia Cranston and Carey Williams" (book review). *Journal of the American Society for Psychical Research,* April 1988.
Angeles, Peter A., *Dictionary of Philosophy.* New York: Barnes and Noble, 1981.
Apfel, Necia H., *It's All Relative.* New York: William Morrow, 1981.
Ariès, Philippe, *The Hour of Our Death.* Transl. by Helen Weaver. New York: Alfred A. Knopf, 1981.

Ashby, Robert H., *The Guidebook for the Study of Psychical Research.* New York: Samuel Weiser, 1972.
Atwater, P. M. H., *Coming Back to Life.* New York: Dodd, Mead, 1988.
Augros, Robert, and George Stanciu, *The New Biology.* Boston: Shambhala, 1987.
Badham, Paul, *Christian Beliefs about Life after Death.* New York: Harper & Row, 1976.
Bagne, Paul, and Nancy Lucas, "Souls on Ice: Cryo Science." *Omni,* October 1986.
Bangs, Richard, and Christian Kallen, *Islands of Fire, Islands of Spice.* San Francisco: Sierra Club Books, 1988.
Barrett, William, *Death of the Soul.* Garden City, N.Y.: Doubleday, 1987.
Baskin, Yvonne, "Roger Sperry." *Omni,* August 1983.
Bateson, Gregory, and Mary Catherine Bateson, *Angels Fear.* New York: Macmillan, 1987.
Beauchamp, Tom L., and LeRoy Walters, eds., *Contemporary Issues in Bioethics.* Belmont, Calif.: Wadsworth, 1989.
Berger, Arthur S., *Aristocracy of the Dead.* Jefferson, N.C.: McFarland, 1987.
Bettman, Otto L., *Pictoral History of Medicine.* Springfield, Ill.: Charles C. Thomas, 1956.
Blackmore, Susan, "Remembering or Self-Remembering: An Essay Review of Charles Tart's Waking-Up—Overcoming the Obstacles to Human Potential." *Journal of the Society for Psychical Research,* October 1987.
Bohm, David J.:
"A New Theory of the Relationship of Mind and Matter." *Journal of the American Society for Psychical Research,* April 1956.
Wholeness and the Implicate Order. London: Routledge & Kegan Paul, 1985.
Brandon, S. G. F., *The Judgment of the Dead.* New York: Charles Scribner's Sons, 1967.
Braude, Stephen E., "Handbook of States of Consciousness, edited by Benjamin B. Wolman and Montague Ullman" (book review). *Journal of the American Society for Psychical Research,* April 1988.
Bucke, Richard Maurice, *Cosmic Consciousness.* New York: E. P. Dutton, 1973.
Burt, Cyril, *ESP and Psychology.* Ed. by Anita Gregory. New York: John Wiles & Sons, 1975.
Capra, Fritjof:
The Tao of Physics. New York: Bantam Books, 1975.
Uncommon Wisdom. New York: Simon & Schuster, 1988.
Casselman, Robert C., *Continuum.* New York: Richard Marek, 1978.
Cassirer, Ernst, *Kant's Life and Thought.* New Haven, Conn.: Yale University Press, 1981.

Cassirer, Manfred, "The Ghost of C. S. Lewis." *Journal of the Society for Psychical Research,* January 1988.

Cavendish, Richard, ed., *Man, Myth & Magic.* New York: Marshall Cavendish, 1983.

Chada, N. K., and Ian Stevenson, "Two Correlates of Violent Death in Cases of the Reincarnation Type." *Journal of the Society for Psychical Research,* April 1988.

Changeaux, Jean-Pierre, *Neuronal Man.* Transl. by Dr. Laurence Carey. New York: Oxford University Press, 1985.

Christopher, Milbourne, *Search for the Soul.* New York: Thomas Y. Crowell, 1979.

Cole, K. C., *Sympathetic Vibrations: Reflections on Physics as a Way of Life.* New York: William Morrow, 1985.

Cook, Emily Williams, "The Survival Question." *Journal of the American Society for Psychical Research,* April 1987.

Copleston, Frederick, *A History of Philosophy.* Vols. 4-6. Garden City, N.Y.: Doubleday, 1985.

Cummins, Geraldine, *Swan on a Black Sea.* Ed. by Signe Toksvig. London: Routledge & Kegan Paul, 1965.

Davidson, Gustav, *A Dictionary of Angels.* New York: The Free Press, 1967.

Davidson, H. R. Ellis, *The Journey to the Other World.* Totowa, N.J.: Rowman and Littlefield, 1975.

Davies, Paul:
   The Cosmic Blueprint. New York: Simon & Schuster, 1988.
   God and the New Physics. New York: Simon & Schuster, 1983.

Davis, Andrew Jackson, *Death and the After-Life.* Boston: William White, 1871.

Dempsey, David, *The Way We Die.* New York: Macmillan, 1975.

Donnelly, John, ed., *Language, Metaphysics, and Death.* New York: Fordham University Press, 1978.

Ducasse, C. J.:
   A Critical Examination of the Belief in a Life after Death. Springfield, Ill.: Charles C. Thomas, 1961.
   Nature, Mind, and Death. La Salle, Ill.: Open Court, 1951.

Eccles, John C.:
   The Human Mystery. New York: Springer International, 1979.
   The Human Psyche. Heidelberg, West Germany: Springer-Verlag, 1980.
   The Wonder of Being Human. New York: Macmillan, 1984.

Eddington, A. S., *The Nature of the Physical World.* New York: Macmillan, 1929.

Edelhart, Michael, "Robo-Psychology," *Omni,* April 1983.

Edwards, Paul, ed., *The Encyclopedia of Philosophy.* Vol. 2. New York: Macmillan, 1967.

Ehrenwald, Jan, M. D., *The ESP Experience.* New York: Basic Books, 1978.

Eisenberg, Howard, *Inner Spaces.* Don Mills, Ontario, Canada: General Publishing, 1977.

Eisenbud, Jule, *Parapsychology and the Unconscious.* Berkeley, Calif.: North Atlantic Books, 1983.

Eliade, Mircea, ed., *The Encyclopedia of Religion.* New York: Macmillan, 1988.

Ellis, William, *The Idea of the Soul in Western Philosophy and Science.* London: George Allen and Unwin, 1940.

d'Espagnat, Bernard, "The Quantum Theory and Reality." *Scientific American,* November 1979.

Evans, C. O., *The Subject of Consciousness.* London: George Allen and Unwin, 1970.

Fletcher, John, *Art Inspired by Rudolf Steiner.* Hertfordshire, England: Mercury Arts, 1987.

Flew, Antony, ed, *Body, Mind, and Death.* New York: Macmillan, 1964.

Flower, Elizabeth, and Murray G. Murphey, *A History of Philosophy in America.* Vol. 1. New York: G. P. Putnam's Sons, 1977.

Fodor, Jerry A., "The Mind-Body Problem." *Scientific American,* January 1981.

French, Peter A., ed., *Philosophers in Wonderland.* St. Paul, Minn.: Llewellyn Publications, 1975.

Friedländer, Paul, *Plato.* Transl. by Hans Meyerhoff. Vol. 1. Princeton, N.J.: Princeton University Press, 1969.

Fuller, John G., *The Great Soul Trial.* New York: Macmillan, 1969.

Gallup, George, Jr., with William Proctor, *Adventures in Immortality.* New York: McGraw Hill, 1982.

Gardner, Martin, "Parapsychology and Quantum Mechanics." In *Science and the Paranormal,* ed. by George O. Abell and Barry Singer. New York: Charles Scribner's Sons, 1983.

Garrison, Webb, *Strange Facts about Death.* Nashville, Tenn.: Abingdon, 1978.

Gauld, Alan, *Mediumship and Survival.* London: Granada, 1982.

Gilling, Dick, and Robin Brightwell, *The Human Brain.* New York: Facts on File, 1982.

Gliedman, John:
   "The Josephson Junction." *Omni,* July 1982.
   "Scientists in Search of the Soul." *Science Digest,* Vol. 90, Issue 7.

Gold, E. J., *American Book of the Dead.* San Francisco: And/Or Press, 1975.

Grant, Patrick, *Literature of Mysticism in Western Tradition.* New York: St. Martin's Press, 1983.

Grattan-Guinnes, Ivor, ed., *Psychical Research.* Wellingborough, Northamptonshire, England: Aquarian Press, 1982.

Greene, F. Gordon, "*Heading Toward Omega,* by Kenneth Ring" (book review). *Journal of the American Society for Psychical Research,* January 1987.

Gregory, Richard L., ed., *The Oxford Companion to the Mind.* Oxford: Oxford University Press, 1987.

Gribbin, John, *In Search of Schrödinger's Cat.* New York: Bantam Books, 1984.

Grosso, Michael:
   The Final Choice. Walpole, N.H.: Stillpoint, 1985.
   "*Precognition and the Philosophy of Science,* by B. Brier" (book review). *Journal of the American Society for Psychical Research,* July 1975.
   "The Survival of Personality in a Mind-Dependent World." *Journal of the American Society for Psychical Research,* October 1979.

Grun, Bernard, *The Timetables of History.* New York: Simon & Schuster, 1982.

Hamblin, Dora Jane, "Strange Quest of James Kidd." *LIFE,* March 3, 1967.

Hansel, C. E. M., *ESP.* New York: Charles Scribner's Sons, 1966.

Haraldsson, Erlendur, *Modern Miracles.* New York: Fawcett Columbine, 1987.

Haraldsson, Erlendur, and Ian Stevenson, "A Communicator of the 'Drop In' Type in Iceland." *Journal of the American Society for Psychical Research,* July 1975.

Hardt, Dale V., *Death: The Final Frontier.* Englewood Cliffs, N.J.: Prentice-Hall, 1979.

Hare, Peter H., and Edward H. Madden, *Causing, Perceiving and Believing.* Boston: D. Reidel, 1975.

Hare, R. M., *Plato.* Oxford: Oxford University Press, 1982.

Harper, George Mills, *The Neoplatonism of William Blake.* Chapel Hill, N.C.: University of North Carolina Press, 1961.

Hart, Hornell, *The Enigma of Survival.* London: Rider, 1959.

Harth, Erich, *Windows on the Mind.* New York: William Morrow, 1982.

Hemleben, Johannes, *Rudolf Steiner.* Transl. by Leo Twyman. East Grinstead, Sussex, England: Henry Goulden, 1975.

Herbert, Nick, *Quantum Reality.* New York: Doubleday, 1985.

Herzog, Edgar, *Psyche and Death.* Transl. by David Cox and Eugene Rolfe. New York: G. P. Putnam's Sons, 1966.

Hildegard of Bingen and Matthew Fox, *Illuminations of Hildegard of Bingen.* Santa Fe, N.M.: Bear & Co., 1985.

Hofstadter, Douglas R.:
   Gödel, Escher, Bach. New York: Basic Books, 1979.
   Metamagical Themas. New York: Basic Books, 1985.

Hooper, Judith, and Dick Teresi, *The Three-Pound Universe.* New York: Dell, 1986.

Hyslop, James H., *Contact with the Other World.* New York: The Century Co., 1919.

Jacobson, Helmuth, Marie-Louise von Franz, and Siegmond Hurwitz, *Timeless Documents of the Soul.* Evanston, Ill.: Northwestern University Press, 1968.

Jacobson, Nils O., *Life without Death?* Transl. by Sheila La Farge. New York: Dell, 1974.

Jaffé, Aniela, *Apparitions.* Irving, Tex.: Spring Publications, 1978.

Jahn, Robert G., and Brenda J. Dunne, *Margins of Reality.* New York: Harcourt Brace Jovanovich, 1987.

Johnson, Martin, "A Technique for Testing the Psi-Field Theory and Some Implications for Survival Research." Parts 1 & 2. *Journal of the Society for Psychical Research,* October 1983 and February 1984.

Jung, C. G.:
   Memories, Dreams, Reflections. Ed. by Aniela Jaffé. New York: Random House, 1965.
   Psychology and Alchemy. Translated by R. F. C. Hull. New York: Pantheon Books, 1953.

Kauvar, Gerald B., and Gerald C. Sorensen, eds., *The Victorian Mind.* New York: G. P. Putnam's Sons, 1969.

Koestler, Arthur, *The Roots of Coincidence.* New York: Random House, 1973.

Korein, Julius, ed., *Brain Death.* New York: New York Academy of Sciences, 1978.

Küng, Hans, *Eternal Life?* Transl. by Edward Quinn. Garden City, N.Y.: Doubleday, 1984.

LaCalle, Trula Michaels, *Voices.* New York: Dodd, Mead, 1987.

Laird, John, *The Idea of the Soul.* Freeport, N.Y.: Books for Libraries Press, 1970 (reprint of 1924 edition).

Lamont, Corliss, *The Illusion of Immortality.* New York: Frederick Ungar, 1965.

Lattimore, Richard, transl., *The Iliad of Homer.* Chicago: University of Chicago Press, 1951.

Lavine, T. Z., *From Socrates to Sartre.* New York: Bantam Books, 1984.

LeShan, Lawrence:
   Alternate Realities. New York: Random House, 1976.
   From Newton to ESP. Wellingborough, Northamptonshire, England: Turnstone Press, 1984.
   The Science of the Paranormal. Wellingborough, Northamptonshire, England: Aquarian Press, 1987.

Lewin, Roger, "Is Your Brain Really Necessary?" *Science,* December 1980.

Lewis, Hywel D., *The Self and Immortality.* New York: Seabury Press, 1973.

Lodge, Oliver J.:
   Raymond. New York: George H. Doran, 1916.

Raymond Revised. London: Methuen, 1922.

Lorimer, David, *Survival?* London: Routledge & Kegan Paul, 1984.

Lowry, Katherine, "Death Avengers." *Omni*, October 1986.

Loye, David, *The Sphinx and the Rainbow*. Boulder, Colo.: Shambhala, 1983.

Lueras, Leonard, *Bali*. Singapore: Times Editions, 1987.

Lund, David H., *Death and Consciousness*. Jefferson, N.C.: McFarland, 1985.

Lundahl, Craig R., comp., *A Collection of Near-Death Research Readings*. Chicago: Nelson-Hall, 1982.

McConnell, R. A., ed., *Encounters with Parapsychology*. Pittsburgh, Pa.: Privately published, 1981.

MacGregor, Geddes, ed., *Immortality and Human Destiny: A Variety of Views*. New York: Paragon House, 1985.

Macintyre, Michael, *Spirit of Asia*. London: British Broadcasting Corp., 1980.

McKinney, H. Lewis, *Wallace and Natural Selection*. New Haven, Conn.: Yale University Press, 1972.

McKnight, Floyd, *Rudolf Steiner and Anthroposophy*. New York: Anthroposophical Society in America, 1977.

Malcolm, Norman, *Ludwig Wittgenstein*. London: Oxford University Press, 1966.

Meyer, Pamela, and Alfred Meyer, "Life and Death in Tana Toradja." *National Geographic*, June 1972

Miller, David, ed., *Popper Selections*. Princeton, N.J.: Princeton University Press, 1985.

Mindell, Arnold, *Dreambody*. Ed. by Sisa Sternback-Scott and Becky Goodman. Santa Monica, Calif.: Sigo Press, 1982.

Moore, Brooke Noel, *The Philosophical Possibilities beyond Death*. Springfield, Ill.: Charles C. Thomas, 1981.

Moore, E. Garth, "Survival: A Reconsideration." *London Society for Psychical Research*, 1966.

Murphy, Gardner, "A Caringtonian Approach to Ian Stevenson's *Twenty Cases Suggestive of Reincarnation*." *Journal of the American Society for Psychical Research*, April 1973.

Murphy, Gardner, and Robert O. Ballou, eds. and comps., *William James on Psychical Research*. New York: Viking Press, 1960.

Murphy, Lois Barclay, "The Evolution of Gardner Murphy's Thinking in Psychology and Psychical Research." *Journal of the American Society for Psychical Research*, April 1988.

"Obituary and Tributes to Curt John Ducasse." *Journal of the American Society for Psychical Research*, April 1970.

Oppenheim, Janet, *The Other World*. Cambridge: Cambridge University Press, 1985.

Ornstein, Robert, ed., *The Nature of Human Consciousness*. New York: Viking Press, 1973.

Ornstein, Robert, and Richard F. Thompson, *The Amazing Brain*. Boston: Houghton Mifflin, 1984.

Osis, Karlis, "Deathbed Observations by Physicans and Nurses." *Journal of the American Society for Psychical Research*, July 1977.

Osis, Karlis, and Erlendur Haraldsson, *At the Hour of Death*. New York: Avon Books, 1977.

Parker-Rhodes, Frederick, "Body, Mind and Soul." *Journal of the Society for Psychical Research*, December 1979.

Pearce-Higgins, Canon J. D., and G. Stanley Whitby, eds., *Life, Death and Psychical Research*. London: Rider, 1973.

Peat, F. David, *Synchronicity*. New York: Bantam Books, 1987.

Pöppel, Ernst, *Mindworks*. Transl. by Tom Artin. Boston: Harcourt Brace Jovanovich, 1988.

Progoff, Ira, transl., *The Cloud of Unknowing*. New York: Julian Press, 1957.

Rawlings, Maurice, *Beyond Death's Door*. Nashville, Tenn.: Thomas Nelson, 1978.

"Researchers Aided by Hermit's Will Fail to Find a Soul." *The New York Times*, June 16, 1975.

Restak, Richard M., M.D.:
The Brain. New York: Bantam Books, 1984.
The Mind. New York: Bantam Books, 1988.

Richmond, Zoë, *Evidence of Purpose*. London: G. Bell & Sons, 1938.

Rogo, D. Scott:
The Infinite Boundary. New York: Dodd, Mead, 1987.
Life after Death. Wellingborough, Northamptonshire, England: Aquarian Press, 1986.
"Survival Research: Problems and Possibilities." *Theta*, winter/spring 1984.

Roll, William G., "The Final Choice: Playing the Survival Game, by Michael Grosso" (book review). *Journal of the American Society for Psychical Research*, April 1988.

Roy, Archie:
"Not Like Her At All." *The Unexplained* (London), Vol. 11, Issue 122.
"The Phantom Universe." *The Unexplained* (London), Vol. 4, Issue 43.

Ryle, Gilbert, *The Concept of Mind*. Chicago: University of Chicago Press, 1984.

Sabom, Michael B., *Recollections of Death*. New York: Harper & Row, 1982.

Sayre, Kenneth M., *Cybernetics and the Philosophy of Mind*. Atlantic Highlands, N.J.: Humanities Press, 1976.

Sheldrake, Rupert, *A New Science of Life*. Los Angeles: J. P. Tarcher, 1981.

Shepard, Leslie, ed., *Encyclopedia of Occultism and Parapsychology*. Detroit, Mich.: Gale Research, 1984.

Sheskin, Arlene, *Cryonics*. New York: Irvington Publishers, 1979.

Shimony, Abner, "The Reality of the Quantum World." *Scientific American*, January 1988.

Shore, Steven N., "Quantum Theory and the Paranormal." *The Skeptical Inquirer*, fall 1984.

Siegel, Ronald K., "Long Day's Journey into Fright." *Omni*, December 1988.

Simpson, Jacqueline, *European Mythology*. New York: Peter Bedrick Books, 1987.

Snow, C. P., *The Physicists*. Boston: Little, Brown, 1981.

Spraggett, Allen, *The Case for Immortality*. New York: New American Library, 1974.

Steiner, Rudolf, *Life between Death and Rebirth*. Transl. by R. M. Querido. Hudson, N.Y.: Anthroposophic Press, 1968.

Stevenson, Ian:
"The Case of Robert Marie: An Additional Note." *Journal of the American Society for Psychical Research*, April 1975.
"The Combination Lock Test for Survival." *Journal of the American Society for Psychical Research*, July 1968.
"A Communicator of the 'Drop In' Type in France: The Case of Robert Marie." *Journal of the American Society for Psychical Research*, January 1973.
"A Communicator Unknown to Medium and Sitters." *Journal of the American Society for Psychical Research*, January 1970.
"Some Questions Related in Cases of the Reincarnation Type." *Journal of the American Society for Psychical Research*, October 1974.
Twenty Cases Suggestive of Reincarnation. Charlottesville, Va.: University Press of Virginia, 1974.

Stevenson, Ian, and John Beloff, "An Analysis of Some Suspect Drop-In Communications." *Journal of the Society for Psychical Research*, September 1980.

Stevenson, Ian, Satwant Paricha, and Godwin Samararatne, "Deception and Self-Deception in Cases of the Reincarnation Type." *Journal of the American Society for Psychical Research*, January 1988.

Swedenborg, Emanuel, *Heaven and Hell*. Transl. by George F. Dole. New York: Pillar Books, 1976.

Talbot, Michael, *Beyond the Quantum*. New York: Macmillan, 1986.

Thouless, Robert H.:
"Do We Survive Bodily Death?" *Proceedings of the Society for Psychical Research*, October 1984.
From Anecdote to Experiment in Psychical Research. London: Routledge & Kegan Paul, 1972.
"Theories about Survival." *Journal of the Society for Psychical Research*, March 1979.

Toynbee, Arnold, et al., *Man's Concern with Death*. St. Louis, Mo.: McGraw-Hill, 1968.

Toynbee, J. M. C., *Death and Burial in the Roman World*. London: Thames and Hudson, 1971.

Turner, Ann Warren, *Houses for the Dead*. New York: David McKay, 1976.

"Update on Thouless Cipher Test of Survival." *Journal of the American Society for Psychical Research*, July 1985.

Valle, Ronald S., and Rolf von Eckartsberg, eds., *The Metaphors of Consciousness*. New York: Plenum Press, 1981.

Van Pearson, C. A., *Body, Soul, Spirit*. Transl. by Hubert H. Hoskins. London: Oxford University Press, 1966.

Vesey, G. N. A., ed., *Body and Mind*. London: George Allen and Unwin, 1964.

Vogel, Shawna, "Cold Storage." *Discover*, February 1988.

Vrooman, Jack Rochford, *René Descartes*. New York: G. P. Putnam's Sons, 1970.

Warthin, Aldred Scott, *The Physician of the Dance of Death*. New York: Arno Press, 1977.

Weintraub, P., "Richard Cutler Interview." *Omni*, October 1986.

Weiss, Brian L., M.D., *Many Lives, Many Masters*. New York: Simon & Schuster, 1988.

Wheatley, James M. O.:
"Between Science and Religion, by Frank M. Turner" (book review). *Journal of the American Society for Psychical Research*, April 1975.
"Love, Telepathy, Survival." *Journal of the American Society for Psychical Research*, July 1973.

Wheatley, James M. O., ed., and Hoyt L. Edge, *Philosophical Dimensions of Parapsychology*. Springfield, Ill.: Charles C. Thomas, 1976.

Wheeler, L. Richmond, *Vitalism*. London: H. F. & G. Witherby, 1989.

White, John, ed., *Frontiers of Consciousness*. New York: Crown, 1974.

White, Rhea A., "Eileen Garrett and the World beyond the Senses, by Allan Angoff" (book review). *Journal of the American Society for Psychical Research*, April 1975.

Who's Who 1983-1984. New York: St. Martin's Press, 1983.

Wilber, Ken:
Eye to Eye. Garden City, N.Y.: Doubleday, 1983.
No Boundary. Boulder, Colo.: Shambhala, 1981.
Transformations of Consciousness. Boulder, Colo.: Shambhala, 1986.

Wolf, Fred Alan, *Taking the Quantum Leap*. San Francisco: Harper & Row, 1981.

Zaleski, Carol, *Otherworld Journeys*. New York: Oxford University Press, 1987.

Zukav, Gary, *The Dancing Wu Li Masters*. New York: Bantam Books, 1979.

INDEX

Time-Life Books Inc.
is a wholly owned subsidiary of
TIME INCORPORATED

Editor-in-Chief: Jason McManus
Chairman and Chief Executive Officer: J. Richard Munro
President and Chief Operating Officer: N. J. Nicholas, Jr.
Editorial Director: Richard B. Stolley

THE TIME INC. BOOK COMPANY
President and Chief Executive Officer: Kelso F. Sutton
President, Time Inc. Books Direct: Christopher T. Linen

TIME-LIFE BOOKS INC.

EDITOR: George Constable
Executive Editor: Ellen Phillips
Director of Design: Louis Klein
Director of Editorial Resources: Phyllis K. Wise
Editorial Board: Russell B. Adams, Jr., Dale M. Brown,
Roberta Conlan, Thomas H. Flaherty, Lee Hassig,
Donia Ann Steele, Rosalind Stubenberg
Director of Photography and Research:
John Conrad Weiser
Assistant Director of Editorial Resources: Elise Ritter Gibson

PRESIDENT: John M. Fahey, Jr.
Senior Vice Presidents: Robert M. DeSena, James L. Mercer,
Paul R. Stewart, Joseph J. Ward
Vice Presidents: Stephen L. Bair, Stephen L. Goldstein,
Juanita T. James, Andrew P. Kaplan, Carol Kaplan,
Susan J. Maruyama, Robert H. Smith
Supervisor of Quality Control: James King

PUBLISHER: Joseph J. Ward

Editorial Operations
Copy Chief: Diane Ullius
Production: Celia Beattie
Library: Louise D. Forstall

Library of Congress Cataloging in Publication Data
Search for the Soul / the editors of Time-Life Books.
  p. cm. — (Mysteries of the unknown)
  Bibliography: p.
  Includes index.
  ISBN 0-8094-6360-1. ISBN 0-8094-6361-X (lib. bdg.)
  1. Soul. 2. Future life.
  I. Time-Life Books. II. Series.
  BD421.S42 1989   89-4612
  128'.1—dc20   CIP

MYSTERIES OF THE UNKNOWN

SERIES DIRECTOR: Russell B. Adams, Jr.
Series Administrator: Myrna Traylor-Herndon
Designer: Susan K. White

Editorial Staff for *Search for the Soul*
Associate Editors: Sara Schneidman (pictures),
Laura Foreman (text)
Text Editor: Janet Cave
Researchers: Christian D. Kinney, Philip M. Murphy
Staff Writer: Marfé Ferguson Delano
Assistant Designer: Susan M. Gibas
Copy Coordinators: Mary Beth Oelkers-Keegan,
Jarelle S. Stein
Picture Coordinator: Ruth J. Moss
Editorial Assistant: Donna Fountain

Special Contributors: Lesley Coleman, Christine Hinze
(London, picture research); Mary Ford Dreesen (lead
research); Beth De Francis, Logan Johnson, Sheila Greene,
Gregory McGruder, Ruth J. Moss, Patricia A. Paterno,
Cornelia M. Piper (research); Grace-Marie Arnett, Sarah
Brash, Kitty Dumas, Dònal Kevin Gordon, Lydia Preston
Hicks, Larry Kahaner, Wendy Murphy, Charles C. Smith,
Daniel Stashower, W. Jere Van Dyk, Bryce S. Walker
(text); John Drummond (design); Hazel Blumberg-McKee
(index)

Correspondents: Elisabeth Kraemer-Singh (Bonn), Vanessa
Kramer (London), Christina Lieberman (New York), Maria
Vincenza Aloisi (Paris), Ann Natanson (Rome).
Valuable assistance was also provided by Mirka Gondicas
(Athens); Angelika Lemmer (Bonn); Judy Aspinall
(London); Simmi Dhanda, Amrita Shah (New Delhi);
Elizabeth Brown, Ann Wise (Rome); Lawrence Chang
(Taipei).

The Consultants:

Marcello Truzzi, professor of sociology at Eastern
Michigan University, is also director of the Center for
Scientific Anomalies Research (CSAR) and editor of its
journal, the *Zetetic Scholar.* Dr. Truzzi, who considers
himself a "constructive skeptic" with regard to claims of
the paranormal, works through the CSAR to produce
dialogues between critics and proponents of unusual
scientific claims.

Brenda J. Dunne is a psychologist and manager of the
Princeton Engineering Anomalies Research laboratory.
She is coauthor with Robert G. Jahn of *Margins of Reality,*
a book that explores the role of human consciousness in
the material world.

Robert G. Jahn is a professor of aerospace sciences and
dean emeritus of the School of Engineering and Applied
Science at Princeton University. With Brenda Dunne, he
has done extensive research on the relationship between
consciousness and matter.

Thelma Z. Lavine is the Clarence B. Robinson Professor of
philosophy and American culture at George Mason University. Her numerous publications include the book *History and Anti-History in Philosophy.* Dr. Lavine also wrote
and presented the Public Broadcasting System television
series "From Socrates to Sartre," based on another of
her books.

William G. Roll, a professor of psychology and psychic
research at West Georgia College, is the founder of the
Psychical Research Foundation and the editor of its
publication, *Theta* magazine. He is among modern parapsychology's leading researchers and theorists.

Other Publications:

AMERICAN COUNTRY
VOYAGE THROUGH THE UNIVERSE
THE THIRD REICH
THE TIME-LIFE GARDENER'S GUIDE
TIME FRAME
FIX IT YOURSELF
FITNESS, HEALTH & NUTRITION
SUCCESSFUL PARENTING
HEALTHY HOME COOKING
UNDERSTANDING COMPUTERS
LIBRARY OF NATIONS
THE ENCHANTED WORLD
THE KODAK LIBRARY OF CREATIVE PHOTOGRAPHY
GREAT MEALS IN MINUTES
THE CIVIL WAR
PLANET EARTH
COLLECTOR'S LIBRARY OF THE CIVIL WAR
THE EPIC OF FLIGHT
THE GOOD COOK
WORLD WAR II
HOME REPAIR AND IMPROVEMENT
THE OLD WEST

*For information on and a full description of any of the Time-
Life Books series listed above, please call 1-800-621-7026
or write:*
Reader Information
Time-Life Customer Service
P.O. Box C-32068
Richmond, Virginia 23261-2068

This volume is one of a series that examines the history
and nature of seemingly paranormal phenomena. Other
books in the series include:
*Mystic Places   Mind over Matter
Psychic Powers   Cosmic Connections
The UFO Phenomenon   Spirit Summonings
Psychic Voyages   Ancient Wisdom and Secret Sects
Phantom Encounters   Hauntings
Visions and Prophecies Powers of Healing
Mysterious Creatures*

Time-Life Books Inc. offers a wide range of fine record-
ings, including a *Rock 'n' Roll Era* series. For subscription
information, call 1-800-621-7026 or write Time-Life
Music, P.O. Box C-32068, Richmond, Virginia 23261-2068.